Ulrike Becker
Managing Challenging Behaviour in Schools

Educational Insights:
Bridging Practice and Research

Volume 5

Pädagogische Einsichten: Praxis und
Wissenschaft im Dialog

Band 5

Ulrike Becker

Managing Challenging Behaviour in Schools

Educational Insights and Interventions

Verlag Barbara Budrich
Opladen • Berlin • Toronto 2025

All rights reserved. No part of this publication may be reproduced, stored in or introduced into a retrieval system, or transmitted, in any form, or by any means (electronic, mechanical, photocopying, recording or otherwise) without the prior written permission of Verlag Barbara Budrich. Any person who does any unauthorized act in relation to this publication may be liable to criminal prosecution and civil claims for damages.

You must not circulate this book in any other binding or cover and you must impose this same condition on any acquirer.

A CIP catalogue record for this book is available from
Die Deutsche Nationalbibliothek (The German National Library):
https://portal.dnb.de.

Carbon compensated production

© 2025   by Verlag Barbara Budrich GmbH, Opladen, Berlin & Toronto

       ISBN   978-3-8474-3107-7 (Paperback)
       eISBN 978-3-8474-3241-8 (PDF)
       eISBN 978-3-8474-3292-0 (EPUB)
       DOI   10.3224/84743107

Verlag Barbara Budrich GmbH
Stauffenbergstr. 7. D-51379 Leverkusen Opladen, Germany | info@budrich.de | www.budrich.de

86 Delma Drive. Toronto, ON M8W 4P6 Canada | info@budrich.de | www.budrich.eu

Cover design by Eva Mutter, Barcelona, using children's drawings made under supervision by visual arts educator Anke Kremer.
Cover images by Annedore Prengel, Anke König, Sophia Richter, and Anne Piezunka.
Typesetting by Anja Borkam, Langenhagen – kontakt@lektorat-borkam.de.
Printed in Europe on FSC®-certified paper by Libri Plureos, Hamburg

Foreword to the small series "Educational Insights: Practice and Science in Dialogue"

The series *"Educational Insights: Practice and Science in Dialogue" series* strives to make knowledge gained in everyday educational experiences and in scientific studies known in the education system. The series is based on the educational insight that valuable sources of knowledge are developed in both educational and scientific fields of work. They should be related to each other and made mutually accessible in understandable language. Each of the books contributes to building bridges between practice and theory.

The target groups of the series are students and teachers at universities, universities of applied sciences and technical colleges, people in administration, supervisory and sponsoring functions, teachers and specialists in educational fields of practice as well as professionals working in further education, counselling, administration and education policy.

The cover design expresses something of the aims, as the graphic elements move from practical educational contexts into the world of educational science. Patchworks of drawings by children and young people are used, which were created under the guidance of Anke Kremer, art teacher and founder of the Internet art gallery "Der rote Hahn". We would like to thank Anke Kremer for collecting the pictures and making them available. Each cover in the series shows a different version of the patchwork. Each individual drawing symbolises freedom for personal uniqueness and intrapersonal versatility. Only in their relational interplay do pictorial elements become expressive and meaningful, visualising inescapable existential relationships. By sharing a common space, different drawings symbolise openness to plurality and mutual appreciation.

The editors of the *Educational Insights* series would like to thank the publisher Barbara Budrich and the editor Miriam von Maydell for their spontaneous willingness to publish this book series in their publishing house and for their careful supervision of the process of creating the books. We would also like to thank the publisher's graphic designer Eva Mutter for producing the covers using the patchworks.

Series editors

Prof. Dr. Anke König (Universität Vechta),
Prof. Dr. Anne Piezunka (Goethe-Universität Frankfurt am Main
and Hochschule für Angewandte Pädagogik Berlin)
Prof. Dr. Annedore Prengel (Contact person for the series:
prengel@uni-potsdam.de, Universität Potsdam i.R.
and Goethe-Universität Frankfurt am Main)
Dr. Sophia Richter (Goethe-Universität Frankfurt am Main)

Table of Contents

Introduction 11

1. Education in times of social crisis 14

    1.1 Psychosocial situation of children and adolescents against the background of social crises 14
    1.2 School as a resilience factor 17
        1.2.1 Classroom teaching 18
        1.2.2 (Digital) learning at a distance 20
        1.2.3 Closeness and distance in the educational relationship 21
    1.3 Conclusion 25

2. Pupils with aggressive behaviour: Behaviour towards teachers 26

    2.1 Theoretical considerations 26
    2.2 Educational attitude 30
    2.3 Cuts as solutions in everyday school life 32
        2.3.1 Reset 32
        2.3.2 From confrontation to closing unity 33
        2.3.3 Paradoxical intervention 33
        2.3.4 Redirect 34
        2.3.5 Going out 35
        2.3.6 Safe storage of dangerous objects 35
        2.3.7 Place swap 35
        2.3.8 Individual work order 36
        2.3.9 Time Out 36
        2.3.10 Trigger acoustic signal 37
    2.4 Reparation instead of punishment 37
    2.5 Conclusion 38

3. Pupils harm others 40

    3.1 Theoretical considerations 40
    3.2 Solutions for conflicts in everyday school life 40
        3.2.1 Reactivation of sibling conflicts 40
        3.2.2 Neglect 45
        3.2.3 Bullying 47

	3.2.4	Stigmatisation	48
	3.2.5	Discrimination because of clan family names	49
	3.2.6	Non-compliance with rules of faith	49
3.3	Conclusion		51
4.	**Pupils harm themselves**		**52**
4.1	Theoretical considerations		52
4.2	Solutions for conflicts in everyday school life		53
	4.2.1	Sensory overload	53
	4.2.2	Separation anxiety	54
	4.2.3	Self-harming behaviour such as scratching	56
	4.2.4	Hyperactivity	58
	4.2.5	Individual retreat	59
	4.2.6	Blows to your own body	60
4.3	Conclusion		61
5.	**Parents who are difficult to reach**		**63**
5.1	Legal framework for working with parents		63
5.2	Effect of parents on children's behaviour		64
5.3	Hard to reach parents		64
	5.3.1	Causes of difficult accessibility	64
	5.3.2	Solutions for conversations with parents	68
5.4	Conclusion		74
6.	**Prevention of challenging behaviour and conflicts**		**75**
6.1	Prevention of challenging behaviour		75
6.2	School policy		75
6.3	School rules		77
6.4	Conclusion		79
7.	**Learning accesses for pupils with special needs in their emotional and social development**		**80**
7.1	Inclusive and exclusive currents		80
7.2	Transition project		81
	7.2.1	Theoretical background	81
	7.2.2	Study results	81
	7.2.3	Internal school organisation	82
	7.2.4	Exchange and dissemination	83
7.3	Five learning accesses		86

		7.3.1	Temporary learning group	86
		7.3.2	Inclusive teaching	88
		7.3.3	Counselling in a multi-professional team	89
		7.3.4	Counselling with parents	91
		7.3.5	Cooperation between schools and youth welfare services	93
	7.4	Conclusion		95
8.	Summary and outlook			96
	8.1	Summary		96
	8.2	Outlook		97
Literature				99
Index				113

Introduction

If the behaviour of children or young people at school does not meet the expectations of the adults working there professionally, it is described as challenging. If pupils' behaviour restricts their own learning or development opportunities or endangers themselves or others, intervention is required to protect them and ensure the well-being of all those involved (Becker 2019c, Hurrelmann 2018, Luder 2019, Werning 2015).

This book is aimed at teachers and educational professionals who are confronted with challenging behaviour in the course of their work. It is intended to provide help

- for customised educational action in difficult situations and conflicts,
- for the development of school policies and school regulations for the prevention of challenging behaviour, conflicts and violence,
- for the inclusive support of pupils with impairments in emotional development.

This book brings together the author's professional experience as a teacher, head teacher and researcher as well as findings from socialisation research, psychology and research into special needs and inclusive education. Case studies are presented that are constructed in a realistic way and describe and justify tried and tested solutions for difficult situations in everyday school life. Any similarities with living persons are purely coincidental.

The case studies show how teachers and educational professionals can approach children and young people in difficult educational situations. Some of the case studies presented in this book were selected by the Helga Breuninger Foundation for the filming of *staged videos* for training and further education.

The book was started at the beginning of March 2022, in the middle of the coronavirus pandemic and shortly after the start of the war in Ukraine. The comments on the social background relate primarily to the period from March 2022 to March 2023. During this year, many educators were primarily concerned with the educational challenges resulting from the current social crises. That is why I have prefaced the central theme of this book, *Managing Challenging Behaviour in Schools*, with Chapter 1 *Education in times of social crisis*.

Irrespective of the current social crises, teachers are particularly affected by educational situations in which they are exposed to aggressive behaviour. Chapter 2 is therefore dedicated to understanding such situations on a case-by-case basis. At the same time, ten tools are presented in the form of the *Cuts*, which enable difficult educational situations to be ended quickly.

Chapters 3 and 4 deal with understanding cases of children and young people who harm others or themselves. In these chapters, readers are presented with case-specific solutions.

Teachers and educational professionals often have the impression that parents[1] are difficult for them to reach. However, if children and young people find themselves in emotional distress, counselling with parents is crucial for finding solutions. When conducting joint counselling sessions with parents, appreciation is the key to success. Chapter 5 presents a possible process for designing appreciative counselling sessions with parents.

Chapter 6 is dedicated to the prevention of conflicts and challenging behaviour at school. It provides impulses for shaping life in the school community that can help to promote the well-being of pupils in such a way that conflicts, discrimination and challenging behaviour are reduced to a minimum. The development of a school policy, school rules and classroom management play a key role in this.

In order to support and encourage children and young people with impairments in emotional and social development, space and time are needed for relationship work. Chapter 7 presents how supportive relationships can be formed with the pupils concerned in order to support ego-integration and thus promote learning, well-being and social participation.

In 1998, the author developed the *Transition project* support approach, which has since been successfully implemented in Hamburg, Bremen, Berlin and individual schools in other federal states. This support approach is described in Chapters 7.2 and 7.3.

This QR code takes you to the staged videos of some case studies. They each show the use of a 'cut'. They were produced by the Helga Breuninger Foundation for the training module 'Being present and empathetic when dealing with conflict'.

1. Education in times of social crisis

1.1 Psychosocial situation of children and adolescents against the background of social crises

In recent decades, there have only been a few overall social events in Germany that have been so overwhelming that they have had an impact on the interaction between children, young people and adults (Luhmann 1988a and Nassehi/Nollmann 2016, Nassehi 2022). The coronavirus pandemic, the climate crisis and wars and terror must be mentioned when listing the crises that are currently influencing the way children and young people in Germany grow up. The current war in Ukraine is an example of other armed conflicts in other countries such as Syria, Afghanistan and Iraq. Last but not least, the Middle East conflict must also be mentioned.

In November 2022, around 89 million people worldwide have been forcibly displaced from crisis regions or are refugees, half of whom are under the age of 18 (UNHCR 2023a). Between 2015 and 2017, the Federal Office for Migration and Refugees registered almost 500,000 initial applications for asylum for minors in Germany. In 2018 and 2019, there were around 150,000 and in 2021 there were 73,281 first-time applications for asylum for minors. The age group of 0 to 4-year-olds dominated. An initial application for asylum was made for 38,799 children in this age group. By January 2023, around 17.6 million people had already fled Ukraine (border crossings), around one million of whom live in Germany, including around 350,000 children and young people (Mediendienst Integration 2023, UNHCR 2023a). Of these, 208,897 children and young people had been admitted to schools in Germany by 2 April 2023 (KMK 2023) Many children and young people in Germany are in a difficult life situation after experiencing flight.

The impact of the coronavirus pandemic on social life has been overwhelming and so drastic that it has not only changed the rules for socialising at school due to the coronavirus, but has also influenced interactions between teachers and pupils in particular. Presumably, the behaviour of all actors at school has changed in such a way that anxieties and depressive symptoms are more evident in children, while aggressive and violent behaviour is less frequently perceived by teachers (Becker 2022b). The current situation in society as a whole and the behaviour of pupils and teachers at school are examples of how the three relationships of micro, meso and macro are systemically interconnected (Bronfenbrenner 1981, Luhmann 1988a).

The coronavirus pandemic meant that schools in Germany were closed for an extended period of time for the first time since the Second World War. The results of studies conducted during the coronavirus pandemic show that the suspension of face-to-face teaching has had a major impact on the psychosocial situation of children and young people (Andresen et al. 2020; Andresen et al. 2022; Ravens-Sieberer et al. 2022b). The causes are manifold and range from the restriction of social contacts to an increase in incidents of violence against children and adolescents. The results of statistical analyses and selected scientific studies on the psychosocial situation of children and adolescents are presented below.

Psychosocial situation of children and adolescents

The statistics from the Federal Criminal Police Office (BKA 2021, Maywald 2021) clearly show the extent to which offences against children have increased in Germany in the first year of the pandemic: 152 children were killed by violence, a third more than in the previous year. 115 of them were under the age of six. There were 49,128 cases of child abuse in 2020, an increase of ten per cent compared to the previous year. The number of cases of child abuse rose by 6.8 per cent to over 14,500 cases. The distribution, acquisition, possession and production of sexual abuse images, known as child pornography, increased by 53 per cent to 18,761 cases.

To gain initial international insights into the psychosocial situation of children and young people during the coronavirus pandemic, UNICEF conducted a study in 21 countries in 2020. 19 per cent of participants said they felt depressed and had no interest in activities. In Germany, the proportion was as high as 24 per cent of young people (UNICEF 2021).

A study by the German Youth Institute shows that 82 per cent of families in Germany with stable material and social living conditions were able to cope well with the coronavirus pandemic. In families with social or material problems and conflicts, the figure was only 47 per cent (Langmeyer et al. 2020a, 2020b).

The KIGGS study (Robert Koch Institute 2018) shows that even before the pandemic, 16.9 per cent of children and young people in Germany had mental health problems between 2014 and 2017. In the age groups of 3 to 14-year-olds, 19.1 per cent of boys and 14.5 per cent of girls were affected during this period. Children and young people growing up with a low socio-economic status were twice as likely to show mental health problems.

The COPSY study, in which a total of 2,471 children and adolescents aged 7 to 17 years (including 1,673 aged 11 to 17 years) and around 2,319 legal guardians of children aged 7 to 17 years took part in a total of five surveys, provides an insight into the development of children's well-being during the pandemic (Ravens-Sieberer et al. 2022b, Kaman et al. 2023). The results of the COPSY study found that in the period from December 2020 to January 2021, 30.4 per cent of the children and adolescents surveyed or the children of the parents surveyed showed mental health problems. In December 2020 to the end of January 2021, the figure was 31 per cent (Ravens-Sieberer et al. 2022a). In the third survey period, September and October 2022, the figure was 27 per cent. In the fourth survey period, in February 2022, the respondents made statements indicating that 28.5 per cent of children and adolescents showed mental health problems at that time (Kaman et al. 2023). In the fifth survey period, in October 2022, the figure was 25 per cent (Kaman et al. 2023). The proportion was therefore higher than before the coronavirus pandemic (Kaman et al. 2023).

In the COPSY study, the periods in which the children felt a particularly high level of stress corresponded significantly with the times when there were no face-to-face lessons. The coronavirus pandemic makes it clear how important school is for the well-being of children and young people, as school is an important place for social communication and relationships. Material problems and social conflicts at home can be partially compensated for.

The results of the studies mentioned here lead to the following conclusion: "When difficult living conditions, stressed parents and children in need of support come together, existing disadvantages are exacerbated. During a crisis, the well-being of children depends even more than usual on the living conditions in the family. This is particularly worrying in the context of child protection. The influencing factors in the family increase when children – due to their own infection or due to cases of infection in the daycare centre group or class – have to go into quarantine" (Langmeyer 2020b, 1) [translated by the author].

With the start of the pandemic-related school closures, research into the learning status of pupils has exploded. In an overview published on 10 February 2021, Fickermann and Edelstein present more than 50 studies (Fickermann/Edelstein 2021). The initial results of this research during the coronavirus pandemic assumed that around 20 per cent of children and young people have pandemic-related learning deficits. For this reason, the Federal Ministry of Education and Research launched the federal-state programme *Catching up after coronavirus for children and young people* with funding of two billion euros. The programme started in June 2021 and the project period ends on 30.09.2023.

It can be assumed that the 20 per cent of pupils affected are those who grow up in stressful life situations. This hypothesis is supported by a Dutch study. Engzell, Frey and Verhagen were able to access a sample of 350,000 pupils. In the Netherlands, the school closure lasted eight weeks and the researchers were able to take advantage of the fact that regular national surveys on learning status were conducted before and after the school closure as part of the state education monitoring programme. The results of the Dutch study indicate that pupils made little or no progress in learning at a distance (Engzell/Frey/Verhagen 2020).

To date, research has largely neglected the connection between the psychological situation of learners and the results of learning status surveys (Kamm/Duveneck/Hoffmeister/Becker 2023). In the study by Helbig (Helbig 2021) on the learning status before and during the coronavirus pandemic, it was found that some students only completed a few tasks during the test. The author suspects that this is due to a lack of subject-specific skills and a lack of motivation to learn on the part of the pupils. Research is pending to investigate whether and how anxious and depressive moods in children and young people contribute to the fact that previously acquired knowledge and cognitive skills cannot be demonstrated in learning assessments or class tests.

Challenging behaviour at school during the coronavirus pandemic

In recent decades, teachers have observed an increasing tendency towards challenging behaviour in the classroom. Further training and specialist days on the topics of *behavioural disorders, challenging behaviour* or *behavioural problems* were in demand, and case consultations or supervision sessions were dominated by cases involving violent behaviour by children or young people towards classmates or teachers.

Since the start of the coronavirus pandemic, these issues have taken a back seat. The reduction in challenging behaviour in the classroom is primarily due to the temporary suspension of face-to-face teaching. Even after returning to face-to-face teaching, teachers report that anxious and depressive symptoms tend to be more prominent in children. It can be assumed that aggressive behaviour at school will increase again a few months after the end of the coronavirus pandemic.

Challenging behaviour arises at the micro level in the interaction between teachers and pupils. Institutional effects are assigned to the meso level and influence the behaviour of teachers and pupils. Institutional effects can encourage, reinforce or reduce challenging behaviour.

1.2 School as a resilience factor

During the coronavirus pandemic, pupils temporarily learnt at a distance. This was increasingly done digitally. The results of the Ravens-Sieberer study (2021, 2022a, 2022b and 2022c) show a temporal correlation between the deterioration in the well-being of children and adolescents and the suspension of face-to-face teaching. With the increasing return of face-to-face teaching, the well-being of pupils increases again (Kaman et al. 2023).

On the one hand, the school serves to impart knowledge. However, it is also an important place for social communication and at the same time has an educational mission. In this sub-chapter, I would like to address the following questions: What does face-to-face teaching do to promote the well-being and improve the psychosocial development of children and young people? What are the positive effects of digital learning at a distance?

1.2.1 Classroom teaching

The following sections explain the central functions of face-to-face teaching, which go beyond the educational mandate and primarily concern the educational mandate. The success of face-to-face teaching always depends on how professionally it is organised (Piezunka 2020).

Support and relief function

With the further development of schools into all-day schools, teachers are increasingly taking on a childcare role that enables both parents and guardians to work. In families where there are many conflicts or material poverty, the school also takes on a relieving, compensatory function for children and young people and their parents (Becker 2008, 2019b).

Supply function

Around 20 per cent of children in Germany grow up in poverty. In many poor families, the children's diet is unhealthy or inadequate (Funcke/Menne 2023, Greiner/Batram/Witte 2019, Statistische Ämter des Bundes und der Länder 2022). This not only has an impact on physical development but also on the learning and behaviour of children and young people. This is why the provision of food in schools is very important. In all-day schools or as part of attendance at an after-school care centre, children receive lunch.

Child protection

In 1919, compulsory schooling was realised in Germany (after a long historical precedent) (Ramseger 2019, Tenorth 2019). "With the enforcement of compulsory education for all children, the right to education based on children's rights is applied" (Prengel 2022, 75). Shortly before the start of the coronavirus pandemic, the 100th anniversary of primary school for (almost) all children was celebrated (Lindemann et al. 2020). Compulsory school attendance allows educators to become aware when children have suffered injuries due to domestic abuse, when children are guilt-distanced or show psychological abnormalities. Teachers then call in support systems or report suspected child endangerment to the relevant youth welfare office. The experiences of individual teachers show that the knowledge of this can lead to parents in need showing less abusive behaviour towards their children in difficult parenting situations.

Preparation for life in a pluralistic democracy

At school, children learn that pupils have different opinions and that conflicts can be resolved peacefully. This means that children in primary school can be prepared for life in a pluralistic democracy (Becker 2016a, 2016c; Prengel 2016b, Prengel 2020).

Creating well-being in the community

Social interaction during school trips, excursions, sports activities, break times, celebrations, etc. is very important for children's well-being. This is true for the majority, even if some may feel uncomfortable during community activities because they feel excluded or experience conflicts (Becker 2016a).

Supportive relationships

At school, teachers have the opportunity to offer children and young people supportive and boundary-setting relationships (Scherzinger/Wettstein 2022, Fischer/Richey 2021). They encourage children, strengthen their sense of self-efficacy, their enthusiasm and motivation to learn, and support them in overcoming learning obstacles and resolving conflicts. They listen to children and support them with domestic problems.

The coronavirus pandemic has significantly changed the way children and young people learn and live as schoolchildren. It initially meant that children tended to be catapulted into the role of independent actors in our society. It became socially necessary for them to observe the quarantine and AHA rules (keep their distance, observe hygiene, wear a mask in everyday life) independently of their parents, test themselves with self-tests under supervision, organise their learning independently and learn how to use the internet and social media responsibly. Due to the suspension of face-to-face teaching, children and young people were required to take responsibility for complying with important rules that had previously been imposed on them by adults. The adults at school became experts who imparted knowledge to pupils at a distance. More than in face-to-face lessons, children and young people are required to actively decide for themselves whether or not to accept the learning opportunities. This is probably also one of the reasons why teachers have observed less aggressive or violent behaviour during the coronavirus pandemic. Learners had less reason to rebel against adults at school. Lack of motivation to learn and resistance shifted to families and parents. Learning at a distance offers many opportunities to withdraw, so that aggressive behaviour as an expression of resistance is not necessary.

Digital distance learning can in no way replace face-to-face teaching with the functions described here (Tellisch/Ostermann 2021, Schulz 2021). For education in the future, it is important to optimise distance learning so that it can be used as a useful supplement to face-to-face teaching.

1.2.2 (Digital) learning at a distance

Independent learning has always been an integral part of school (Berg 1991, Führ/Furck 1998, Tenorth 2019, Langewiesche/Tenorth 1989). Homework and preparation for learning assessments require pupils to be self-motivated and self-regulated. Distance learning courses for children from year five who live abroad or for young people with school distance have been around for many years. In addition, digital learning at a distance offers good opportunities for expanding free or project work as part of individual learning. This also implies the possibility of extending individual learning more into the home environment. This includes learning in projects or free work as well as the realisation of practice phases, e.g. when learning vocabulary. This would make more educational sense than the current concepts for homework and would ensure the maintenance and expansion of pupils' digital skills. It may then be possible to dispense with homework altogether.

In everyday school life, supportive relationships between teachers and pupils must be established and practised in presence (Zimmermann 2021, Becker 2019c). Learning at a distance offers many possibilities and also opportunities to supplement the relationships offered in presence. However, the experiences of the coronavirus pandemic show that the technical equipment at schools in Germany is not yet sufficiently good across the board and needs to be expanded.

In order to promote individual learning at a distance, it is of central importance to hold regular, daily or weekly individual feedback sessions with pupils on their learning success. In addition, parents/guardians should be included in the feedback sessions two to three times a year (Senate Department for Education, Youth and Family 2021). As part of the federal-state programme for catching up after corona for children and young people, the state of Berlin has stipulated that in the 2021/2022 school year, every pupil must be offered at least two feedback meetings with parents to accompany the learning process (Senate Department for Education, Youth and Family Berlin 2021).

Distance learning is also practised when children are ill and cannot attend face-to-face lessons. Digital distance learning offers many opportunities as a supplement to face-to-face teaching. Research has so far paid too little attention to the fact that this supplement can be used in a educationally meaningful way to promote pupils' learning development and prevent challenging behaviour. To achieve this, it is necessary to find a good balance between closeness and distance in educational relationships. This is equally important in face-to-face and (digital) distance learning (Becker 1995a, 1995b; Thiersch 2020).

1.2.3 Closeness and distance in the educational relationship

From the perspective of developmental psychology, experiences of distance and separation play an important role in children's development in the context of supportive educational relationships (Becker 1995a, Langnickel 2021). This is described in important works of French psychoanalysis. Lacan and Mannoni refer to Sigmund Freud's *Fort-Da game* (Becker 1995a, Mannoni 1982).

> Fort-Da Game
>
> In Beyond the Pleasure Principle, Freud describes his observations of his 18-month-old grandchild's play and interprets his observations as a *Fort ['gone']-Da ['there'] game:* The child had a wooden reel with a piece of string tied round it. It never occurred to him, to pull it along the floor behind him, for instance, and play at ist being a carriage. What he did was to hold the reel by the string and very skilfully throw it over the edge of his curtained cot, so that it disappeared into it, at the same time uttering his expressive `o-o-o-o`. He then pulled the reel and hailed its reappearance with a joyful `da` [`there`]. This, then, was the complete game – disappearance and return. As a rule one only witnessed its first act, which was repeated untiringly as a game in itself, though there is no doubt that the greater pleasure was attached to the second act. out of the bed again by the string, but now greeted its appearance with a joyful 'there'. So this was the complete play, disappearance and reappearance, of which one usually only saw the first act, and this was tirelessly repeated as a play in itself, although the greater pleasure was undoubtedly attached to the second act" (Freud, S. 1920g, 15).

Freud concludes that the child is sad about the mother's departure and that the mother's departure creates unhappiness in the child. Mannoni (1982) takes up this interpretation in her work on these psychoanalytical findings: the child takes possession of the separation experience, which initially generates unhappiness, by actively repeating it himself. This generates motivation and leads to an inner representation and thus to the symbolisation of the absent object (Becker 1995a).

Mannoni concludes from the work of Freud and Lacan that an emotionally acceptable spatial distance in the context of supportive relationships makes learning processes possible in the first place: learning always takes place between a *Fort ['gone']* and *Da ['there']* (Becker 1995a, 1995b). In the *Fort-Da game* described by Freud, it becomes clear how the temporary absence of the primary caregiver triggers the steps of language development in his grandchild. This example clearly illustrates how important the interplay between closeness and distance is for children's development.

The degree of reasonable or necessary distance varies from person to person and must be constantly readjusted within the school institution in dialogue between teachers and pupils in order to facilitate learning and make challenging behaviour superfluous. Unfortunately, this is often not taken into account in everyday school life. Instead, difficult children require intensive one-to-one support, preferably always sitting right next to the child who is perceived as difficult. Herz, Meyer and Liesebach describe that the greatest increase in the use of integration support has been recorded for pupils with challenging behaviour (Herz/Liesebach/Meyer 2018).

Learning in a educational relationship characterised by a balance between closeness and distance can act as a motor for learning development, the development of language and behaviour (Becker 1995a, Roorda et al. 2017). Pupils can learn more successfully and teachers are less likely to notice challenging behaviour. This takes the pressure off interactions between teachers and pupils. This also supports the health of teachers and educational professionals as well as the well-being of children and young people (Hehn-Oldiges 2021). Embedded in a supportive educational relationship, distance learning can have great potential for the development of children and young people.

If we look at learning formats in schools that already successfully incorporate a good balance between proximity and distance in their design and implementation in everyday life, we can see that they have the following characteristics:

- strong educational relationships
- learning in the classroom and at extracurricular learning locations
- a balance between individual learning and learning in small groups
- *coaching to learn* independent learning at a distance
- presentation of the results of independent learning in the class or school community

Learning formats that already take into account a good balance between closeness and distance are intependant learning, *The Challenge Project*, *Research Days*, *Philosophizing with Children*, interdisciplinary learning (Pech 2018, 2020) and project learning. A new and previously little-known learning format is *Frei Day* (Rasfeld 2021).

Frei Day – a learning format that combines sustainable development and a good balance between closeness and distance

The *Frei Day* learning format was developed by Magret Rasfeld and the Schule im Aufbruch network. The idea of Frei *Day* enables children and young people to learn and work independently on topics relating to the world of tomorrow based on their interests. The background to this is the United Nations 2030 Agenda with 17 goals for sustainable development, which Engagement global has prepared for educational purposes on behalf of the Federal Ministry for

Economic Cooperation and Development (Engagement global 2022). The goals revolve around topics such as climate change and environmental protection, hunger, poverty, the unfair distribution of resources and peacekeeping.

On *Frei Day*, pupils learn in a participatory, independent and responsible way. They are challenged to form their own opinions and learn co-determination and self-determination. The *Frei Day* concept is therefore not only linked to the 2030 Agenda but also to Articles 12, 13 and 29 of the Convention on the Rights of the Child (UN General Assembly 1989). Article 12 sets out the right to have the will of the child taken into account as well as the right to participation and co-determination. Article 13 focuses on the right to freedom of expression and the right to information.

Article 29 of the UN Convention on the Rights of the Child

States Parties agree that the education of the child shall be directed to:

(a) The development of the child's personality, talents and mental and physical abilities to their fullest potential;
(b) The development of respect for human rights and fundamental freedoms, and for the principles enshrined in the Charter of the United Nations;
(c) The development of respect for the child's parents, his or her own cultural identity, language and values, for the national values of the country in which the child is living, the country from which he or she may originate, and for civilizations different from his or her own;
(d) The preparation of the child for responsible life in a free society, in the spirit of understanding, peace, tolerance, equality of sexes, and friendship among all peoples, ethnic, national and religious groups and persons of indigenous origin;
(e) The development of respect for the natural environment (UNICEF 1989)

The schools use four hours a week to implement the *Frei Day*. *Frei Day* is divided into three phases:

1. Pupils present their project to the class community (or cross-grade community), discuss it with peers and try to win over other stakeholders.
2. Children or young people learn or work on their project individually or in small groups. They use extracurricular learning centres and receive guidance or coaching to learn from adults.
3. The learning processes of the day or week are reflected on in the class community (or inter-year community).

Frey Day implies failure as part of the learning process on each pupil's individual learning path. In such situations, teachers advise the child or young person concerned so that each pupil can overcome such a difficult situation in a stronger way. This is particularly important for children with challenging behaviour, who often show little tolerance for frustration. Learning processes and results of learning on *Frey Day* are regularly presented to the class or school community (Rasfeld 2021).

Creating a good balance between closeness and distance when learning at a distance and in presence

In order for synergies to develop from face-to-face teaching and distance learning, which can be particularly beneficial for children and young people with challenging behaviour, it is important to adhere to the following criteria:

- Learning at a distance or at extracurricular learning locations supplements face-to-face lessons with individual free or project work or replaces conventional concepts of homework.
- Teachers and other educators cultivate supportive relationships with the pupils, which are established and nurtured in classroom situations, in conversations, on excursions, while playing or during the break.
- Teachers conduct a daily or weekly feedback session with each pupil as required to accompany the learning process (chapter 5). This takes five to ten minutes.
- Teachers conduct an individual feedback meeting two to three times a year to accompany the learning process, in which the child's parents or guardians and the child are involved in an age-appropriate manner. The phases of the feedback meeting are Self-reflection by the child, observations by the teacher on the child's learning process, observations by the parents, formulation of the next goal, planning of implementation, reflection on the discussion by the discussion participants.
- The class teacher organises a daily morning ritual with their learning group, which enables the pupils to talk about current concerns, and a weekly class council.
- The teacher conducts classroom discussions with the pupils. Digital media that enable pupils to actively participate in the classroom discussion (concept board, miro board, etc.) are used.
- The teacher evaluates the lesson discussion with the students.
- Films and texts for information supplement the classroom discussion and joint learning.
- The regular use of digital tools to monitor learning progress (such as IleA+, Lernlinie or Quop) supplements the self-perception of pupils and teachers with regard to the learning development of each child.

1.3 Conclusion

Research on the current situation of children and young people as well as the experiences of educators emphasise the particular importance of the institution of school for the healthy development and well-being of children and young people. Educational relationships play a central role in this.

Experience with (digital) distance learning shows that face-to-face teaching cannot be replaced. Face-to-face teaching fulfils six important functions in the education and training of pupils. This is recognised in Germany through compulsory schooling (Prengel 2022, 75).

Digital learning at a distance requires children and young people to take responsibility in the learning process. They become actors and must take responsibility for their own learning. This requires pupils to participate in the teaching process. It also means recognising that they are allowed to disagree with adults, make mistakes and make errors. This change in the role of learners influences the interaction between teachers and pupils to the effect that they communicate with each other as equals. This reduces the occasions for defensiveness and resistance, disruption of lessons and challenging behaviour.

Distance learning can be successfully implemented if it complements face-to-face teaching in a meaningful way and the criteria outlined for promoting wellbeing, community experience and supporting self-efficacy and school success are adhered to. The balance between proximity and distance is of particular importance here. It can be assumed that in such a educational setting, suspensions due to challenging behaviour can be avoided. In fact, learning that is characterised by a good balance between closeness and distance helps to prevent challenging behaviour and promote independent learning.

2. Pupils with aggressive behaviour: Behaviour towards teachers

2.1 Theoretical considerations

In schools and lessons, there are always educational situations in which teachers feel provoked or threatened by a pupil or group of pupils. Such situations usually lead to feelings of powerlessness, helplessness and feelings of powerlessness and helplessness among teachers. In rare individual cases, teachers may also be psychologically or physically harmed by young people.

This chapter deals with children and young people who display aggressive behaviour towards teachers due to impairments in their emotional or social development.

Children or young people can experience teachers as threatening in the classroom. They either feel they are being bullied and devalued by them or they are looking for more attention. It is not uncommon for pupils to oscillate between the two views. For example, a child may feel disadvantaged compared to other children because they are the last to receive a worksheet from the teacher. A child may also feel bullied because the teacher wants to talk to them during the break about the maths methods they have used to solve problems. A child may also feel disadvantaged if they are called on too often by the teacher in class and asked to speak or complain because this happens too rarely. Subjectively experienced discrimination, paternalism or disregard can therefore be causes that trigger aggressive behaviour towards teachers. This can manifest itself in insults, verbal abuse or the throwing of paper balls or objects at the teacher. Sometimes there are also verbal threats of violence or threats with weapons, such as a knife.

Due to the negative consequences for all parties involved, such situations should be prevented. Constructive solutions must be found in conflict situations. In terms of inclusive education, the aim must be to "limit violence instead of marginalising young people" (Auchter 1994, 55) [Translated by the author].

In order to deal with aggressive behaviour towards teachers in an educationally constructive way, a deeper understanding of difficult situations is necessary. The pupil's perception of the situation is the starting point of a conflict, and the aggressive behaviour is an unconscious cry for help from the child or young person to their social environment. Three questions will be pursued in the following:

What are the causes of aggressive behaviour in children and young people who have experienced too few supportive relationships in early childhood? What part do teachers play in difficult educational situations? How can prevention be strengthened through educational action and how can conflicts in the classroom be reduced?

Impairments in early childhood

For healthy emotional development, children need supportive relationships with parents. However, these attachment figures can also be replaced by other adult attachment figures who are permanently available to children when children grow up in adoptive or foster families, with grandparents or in shared flats. Continuous, supportive relationships in early childhood are referred to as primary relationships or attachment (Becker 1995a). Providing support implies the provision of nourishment, the availability of caregivers, protection from physical and emotional injury and the endurance of difficult situations with the child. The following section describes some typical family situations that affect the emotional-social development of children to such an extent that challenging behaviour can occur.

If parents are too preoccupied with their own material or psychological problems, alcohol addiction or drug use, they can only be available to the child as a carer to a limited extent or not at all. Young children then often develop early childhood attachment disorders, while older children often take over parental functions on behalf of their siblings.

When coping with difficult situations with an infant or toddler, problems can also arise if parents are insecure in their role as parents due to their own biographical experiences. It is possible that even loving parents may display behaviour in difficult situations that has a negative impact on a child's emotional development. For example, parents may shake a child if it cries for a long time. Such a situation can arise when parents lose their patience. These are primarily parents who are still unsure or overwhelmed in their role and experience helplessness in their relationship with their child.

This can lead to shaking trauma. Shaking trauma is the most common non-natural cause of death in children (Nationales Zentrum frühe Hilfen, 2022). The number of unreported cases is unknown. Every year, between 100 and 200 children are hospitalised due to shaking trauma. 10 to 20 per cent survive this without consequential damage. 10 to 30 per cent die as a result. 50 to 70 per cent suffer lifelong consequences, such as visual and speech disorders, cognitive learning and developmental delays, seizures or even severe permanent physical and mental impairments (Nationales Zentrum frühe Hilfen 2022).

Children who experience too little emotional support within the primary relationship in their early childhood initially develop little or no ability to empathise with others (Winnicott 2023). They develop unconscious fears and feel powerless. This is why they repeatedly seek support from their primary carers.

If they are unsuccessful, they often defend themselves against their powerlessness and fear through aggressive behaviour. It is also possible for children to withdraw into themselves and show depressive symptoms.

If a parent or guardian is violent towards a child, children can also identify with the parent and behave violently towards others themselves. This makes them feel strong and reduces their fears.

If children with impaired emotional development experience their school as their home, they unconsciously project aspects of their primary caregivers onto teachers. As a result, they feel the powerlessness, fear or anger towards these adults that they have developed in their primary relationships. They may also steal objects that are meaningful to them or the teacher (Becker 1995a, Leber 1983, Gerspach/Katzenbach 1996, Hehn-Oldiges 2021, Katzenbach 2004, Würker 2007, Zimmermann/Würker 2023).

Such behaviour, which is perceived at school as challenging behaviour or an attack on others, represents a desperate cry for emotional support from the professional reference persons The well-known British child and adolescent psychiatrist and psychoanalyst D.W. Winnicott (…) speaks of *delinquency as a sign of hope* (Auchter 1994, Becker 1995a, Winnicott 2023). Teachers cannot replace parents or guardians for children. However, they can provide support and boundaries, which favours children's ego integration and enables them to develop the ability to empathise with others. To this end, it is necessary for teachers not to *intervene* when children or adolescents become challenging and aggressive, but to offer them support (Leber 1983, Gerspach/Katzenbach 1996, Würker 2007, Hehn-Oldiges 2021).

The part of teachers in difficult situations

Teachers' behaviour is shaped by their own personality and biography. These unconscious parts of a teacher's personality come to the fore in the classroom, especially when pupils display challenging behaviour, provoke and push the teacher to their psychological limits.

The pupil unconsciously transfers aspects of their parent's personality to the teacher. This is referred to as *transference*. The pupil's behaviour triggers the teacher's unconscious reaction, which is also based on their biographical experiences. This is called *counter-transference*. The interplay between *transference* and *countertransference* in the classroom is referred to as a *scene* (Becker 1995a, Leber 1983, Gerspach/Katzenbach 1996, Würker 2007, Zimmermann/Würker 2023). Such unconsciously occurring *scenes* can be the trigger for the teacher to demand that a child or adolescent be segregated in a special institution because the situation at school seems hopeless. This is particularly the case if the teacher identifies with the powerlessness of a child due to their own biographical experiences. Teachers then often say: "I no longer know how to help the child. It would certainly be easier to do this in a youth welfare centre or a special school. The teachers there are trained to do that."

This is usually a misjudgement: the teachers do not realise how successfully they are already supporting the pupils concerned in everyday school life. Be it by preparing differentiated work tasks for them, praising them, giving them a pencil or eraser if one is missing, providing drinks, seeking individual dialogue with them or taking them on class trips lasting several days.

For children and adolescents who have experienced too little emotional support in the primary relationship, it is initially very important that the teachers *tolerate* them despite their disruptive behaviour and do not break off the relationship by refusing to teach such a child and demanding that the child be segregated. The behaviour of children that affects teachers or other children must be limited without excluding the child in question (Auchter 1994, 55). This endurance can enable the child to develop the *capacity for concern* (Winnicott 2023). If a child achieves this competence in interaction with a teacher, this leads to feelings of guilt in the event of aggressive behaviour towards the teacher. The attainment of the *capacity for concern* becomes clear to teachers when a child or adolescent shows a tendency to make amends by wanting to repair or replace objects that they have broken or by bringing the teacher concerned a gift, drawing a picture for them or showing unexpected kindness in some other way. Developing the *capacity for concern is* one of the key prerequisites for reducing or eliminating aggressive behaviour in the long term.

Coping with children and young people who are experienced as difficult is of central importance for the development of pupils and at the same time a very rocky and long road for teachers. They need support in the form of teamwork, case counselling, supervision or coaching.

The success of inclusive education in the case of challenging behaviour requires supportive relationships and a setting within the school that allows the effect of supportive relationships to unfold. The following aspects at the institutional and relationship level are particularly important for implementation:

> Relationship level
> - Appreciation, praise and recognition for the child experienced as difficult
> - For aggressive behaviour:
>   - Interruption of *negative transference* to teachers
>   - Self-protection
>   - *Reparation instead of punishment* as a constructive form of conflict resolution
>
> Institutional level
> - A specific setting for support at school (Chapter 7)
> - Class and school rules based on appreciation and recognition
> - Regular supervision or case counselling to understand unconscious scenes between teachers and children
> - Educational support through youth welfare services

2.2 Educational attitude

Appreciation, praise and recognition

Children or adolescents with challenging behaviour often have unconscious anxieties. They feel powerless and their challenging behaviour is a result of these anxieties and feelings of powerlessness. If they receive appreciation, praise and recognition from teachers, this can reduce their anxieties and feelings of powerlessness. This directly results in a reduction in their challenging behaviour, which teachers usually experience as a relief in the classroom.

It is important that the teacher's attitude is characterised by curiosity about a pupil's questions and interest in their contributions and questions. This expresses appreciation and recognition. Praise should be given by the teacher for the effort a child or young person has made to acquire a skill or achieve a goal.

Case study Pedro

Pedro (13) is a pupil with special educational needs and attends year seven at a secondary school. Pedro can read and write simple texts aloud. In maths, he can solve written addition and subtraction problems. Pedro's birth mother was a heroin addict. After he was born, she wanted to kill herself and him together. She died eight months later from a heroin overdose. Since then, he has lived alone with his father in a caravan.

Pedro is small for his age and looks like an eight-year-old boy. Regardless of the time of year, Pedro comes to school dressed in a red T-shirt and a dark blue waistcoat. He is always punctual and often stays on the school grounds after school. He stands out due to his pronounced attachment to his class teacher. Other teachers describe his behaviour as that of a dog that is always close to its master. In the morning circle, he regularly talks about his rabbit, which fell from the fifth floor window onto the garage roof and survived the fall unharmed.

As soon as the teacher or another adult asks Pedro to sit down in class and work in writing, he becomes very restless at his seat. He kicks the table top from below and draws on the table with his pencil in large swings, so that the teacher spontaneously reprimands him and asks him to clean the table. Instead of calming down, he then jumps up and reacts very aggressively to her verbally. The more the teacher insists, the more agitated and aggressive Pedro becomes.

After a day at school, the class teacher starts to clean the table top herself. At this moment, Pedro comes in the door, takes the sponge from her and cleans the table himself. The teacher agrees with Pedro that from now on he will do his written work on a blackboard hanging next to the classroom door. She also discusses with Pedro that they will stretch paper over his table together in the morning before the lesson starts so that he can draw on it. At the end of the lesson, it is to be taken down and placed in an art folder. At the end of the week, she wants to look at the drawings with him and give them a name. Then she would like to choose a picture together with him to hang up in the classroom.

Pedro is a boy who can sense himself through movement and motor activity. He repeatedly talks about the story of the rabbit that survived a dangerous situation. This story is representative of his own life story. It is amazing that he survived the difficult living conditions in his early childhood and his biological mother's attempt to kill him and herself. Due to his hypermotor activity, he always feels that he is alive and safe. If he has to sit still, he is overwhelmed by powerlessness, which he then has to fend off in aggressive behaviour (Becker 2006). The hyperactive and aggressive behaviour can be seen as a survival reaction on his part.

The class teacher recognises his need and offers him other opportunities to take part in lessons. Creating the opportunity to work on the blackboard and paint on the table recognises his elementary need for movement and at the same time enables him to complete school tasks. By displaying his pictures, on which he is labelled as an "artist", the teacher creates evidence of his existence, which has an anxieties-reducing effect on him.

2.3 Cuts as solutions in everyday school life

In everyday school life, children or young people and their teachers often need a break in difficult situations. This should serve to limit aggression and violence and enable teachers to reflect on their educational actions. I call this form of intervention through an interruption a *cut*. I have trialled it over several years in everyday school life and am presenting it here for the first time in a publication. In the following, examples from a series of case studies are used to present various instruments for creating a *cut,* which can be promisingly included in the repertoire of action of every teacher.

2.3.1 Reset

Johann

Johann (15) is late for class. He kicks the door loudly from outside, causing everyone in class to flinch, opens it, enters and loudly slams the door shut again. He is wearing a baseball cap, which is forbidden according to the school rules. Johann stands up physically in front of the teacher and grins at her.

"Good morning Johann! Nice of you to come." The teacher walks past Johann and opens the door with the words: "Reset! Please come in again and follow all the class rules." Johann leaves the room. The teacher closes the door. Johann now knocks quietly, enters and sits down quietly in his seat without his baseball cap.

Johann seeks the teacher's attention with his behaviour. Johann has several siblings. His parents usually watch TV programmes when he is at home and do not react to him when he enters the house. The parents have two large mastiffs that they love very much. The family does not eat meals together. Conversations between Johann and his parents are rare or non-existent. In Johann's experience, his parents only react to him when he loudly enters the home.

At school, he shows the same behaviour towards the teacher that he is successful with at home. In the scene depicted, the teacher does not react to Johann's provocations, but nevertheless gives him her full attention by establishing a relationship with him. She recognises that he has come and sets boundaries within the relationship without excluding him. She does this by ignoring his problematic behaviour and accompanying him as he enters the classroom in compliance with the class rules. As Johann's goal of gaining the teacher's attention is achieved in this way, he is able to respond to the teacher's requests.

2.3.2 From confrontation to closing unity

Mia

Mia (14) is writing *WhatsApp messages* under the table during a class test. The teacher is furious, stands in front of her desk and shouts at her: "Mia, put your mobile phone away immediately." Mia doesn't react. Instead, Mia takes some perfume out of her bag and wants to spray it on the teacher's face.

The teacher steps aside and positions herself at a 90-degree angle to Mia: "You're now afraid of getting a bad mark because you used your mobile phone during class work. I'm going to take your perfume and your mobile phone. I'll keep both for you in your desk until the end of the lesson. Now you finish your work and we'll find a solution together after the lesson." The teacher holds her open hand over Mia's desk and she puts both in it.

After the lesson, the announced discussion takes place. As the teacher suspects, Mia is afraid that her work could be marked as *unsatisfactory* because of the unauthorised use of her mobile phone. The teacher admits that she should have reacted differently to Mia's misbehaviour. After the teacher explains that she is allergic to perfume, Mia apologises. She wants to explain in the next class council meeting why spraying perfume around can be dangerous.

2.3.3 Paradoxical intervention

Sanna

The teacher collects ten euros for each pupil in class 3c for a class excursion and places the tin with the money in her desk in the classroom. As the amount collected is not enough, she adds another 50 euros from her wallet.

During the break, Sanna stays in class to do her sweeping. At the end of the day, the teacher realises that the tin has disappeared. Sanna has stolen small amounts of money several times in recent months. The teacher wants to speak to Sanna, who is still in the classroom, and ask whether she has taken the money or whether another child has come into the classroom while she was alone during the break. She sits down at the table with Sanna. From there, she notices out of the corner of her eye that the tin is sticking out of Sanna's school bag. Sanna tells the teacher that she hasn't seen anyone. When the teacher asks her if she knows where the tin with the money might have gone, she replies: "I don't know!"

The teacher points to the schoolbag and says: "Look! There's the tin." Sanna opens the bag and takes it out. Sanna stammers that she doesn't know how it got there. The teacher builds her a bridge and says: "Did you put it in your bag to look after it?" Sanna nods. The teacher then says: "I would like you to take on the role of class treasurer. This includes collecting the money

33

from the children and keeping a cash book. You have to regularly write down how much money has been collected and spent. In addition, the class cash box must be locked in the cupboard. Keeping an eye on the key is also part of this job." Sanna is very happy about the task and the teacher's trust. This makes Sanna feel emotionally close to her and safe. From then on, money never disappears from the class register again. Sanna carries out her duties responsibly. Sanna is the daughter of alcoholic parents. She no longer has any contact with her father. Sanna grows up alternately with her mother and in residential youth welfare centres, as her mother is unable to look after her permanently due to her alcohol addiction.

Due to the loss of contact with her father, the constantly changing caregivers in the residential youth welfare centres and the lack of continuity in her relationship with her mother, Sanna is unable to develop a primary relationship that provides her with sufficient emotional support. She unconsciously transfers her desire for affection to her teacher. This is reflected in her everyday life in that she often seeks closeness to her teacher. By stealing the money, she takes possession of something valuable that belongs to the teacher (Aichhorn 2005). This allows her to feel close to her without receiving her constant attention. This reduces Sanna's anxieties and her powerlessness. She feels strong. The teacher does not react primarily to the stealing but rather to Sanna's unconscious desire for attention. By giving her the job of cashier, she enables Sanna to feel close to her and safe.

2.3.4 Redirect

Sven and Metin

In geography class, Metin writes an insulting expression on a piece of paper and holds it up so that Sven can read it. Sven (14) jumps up and shouts at Metin. He wants to go after Metin to hit him. The teacher gets in the way and then immediately switches to a position where she is standing at a 90-degree angle to Sven. She says to him: "You're much bigger and stronger than Metin. It's beneath you to beat a weaker man. Let's go to the front. You operate the smartboard while I present the map". Sven turns round and accompanies the teacher.

Sven feels offended because Metin has written a *girl's hairstyle* on a piece of paper and shown it to him. Sven was often mistaken for his twin sister when he was at primary school. Sven was short and slim. He had shoulder-length hair as a primary school child. Now he is tall and strong. He trains in boxing. It is important to Sven to appear masculine and strong to others. At the moment, his hair has grown a little longer again. Metin's *girl's hairstyle* throws him back to the time when he was mistaken for his sister. He reacts to this with anger. The teacher brings him back to the present with her speech and gives him a responsible task. Sven manages to get out of the argument with Metin. The lesson can continue.

During the break, the teacher talks to Metin about his reasons for his provocative behaviour towards Sven. Metin says he didn't feel like doing geography and provoked Sven to disrupt the lesson. Metin apologises to the teacher and agrees to address the issue in the class council and make up with Sven.

2.3.5 Going out

Mr Meyer

Mr Meyer comes into an eighth grade class where he teaches ethics. It is his third lesson in the class. The group does not respond to him. He leaves the room without saying a word and returns a few minutes later. When he enters the room, everyone sits down and waits quietly for the lesson to begin.

2.3.6 Safe storage of dangerous objects

Paul

Paul (13) opens a knife under the table in chemistry class to show it to the person sitting next to him. Janina, who is sitting next to him, quietly tells the teacher. Mr Schwarz sends all the pupils out into the schoolyard in small groups with a work assignment and stays behind with Paul. He sits down at a 90-degree angle to him. Mr Schwarz speaks to Paul and asks him to show him the knife. He explains to Paul at what blade length one speaks of a weapon and suggests measuring the blade length of his knife. Paul likes the suggestion. When measuring, they both realise that the blade is 0.5 cm too short to be a weapon. To avoid any misunderstandings, the teacher suggests that Paul lock the knife in his desk and then store it in the school safe after the lesson so that nothing can happen and, above all, no adult can take it away from him. The parents or guardians can pick it up later.

2.3.7 Place swap

Melanie

Mr Hoffmann teaches history in class 9b. Melanie (14) feels unfairly treated by the marking of a learning objective test. Melanie shouts at Mr Hoffmann and is unable to calm down. She approaches him and tries to get him to react with sexualised behaviour. Mr Hoffmann asks the class representative, who is sitting near him, to fetch the teacher from the next room. The two teachers swap learning groups and the lesson continues. A conflict resolution meeting is scheduled for the same day. The school management or the school social work specialist takes over the dialogue.

2.3.8 Individual work order

Pit

Pit (11) comes to maths class overtired. The topic being taught today is angles. The teacher welcomes him: "Nice of you to come!"

Pit wants to listen to loud music in class to keep himself awake. When the teacher speaks to Pit, he reacts with insults. The teacher knows that Pit lives in a family that often listens to loud music and parties at night. His parents and older siblings often don't go to bed until three o'clock in the morning. The seven siblings sleep on a carpet in a shared room. The teacher recognises that Pit manages to get to school on time.

The teacher gives Pit and two other boys the task of looking for *acute angles* in the school building and counting them. After 15 minutes, they are to return and present their results. By walking around, Pit wakes up and is able to present his results with his two classmates at the end of the lesson.

2.3.9 Time Out

Serkan

Serkan (14) was expelled from school twice because he reacted to instructions from teachers with threats. At the last school he attended, he pushed a teacher several times.

Serkan has his first day at his new school. During the admissions interview, the headteacher asks Serkan how he came to threaten the teachers. Serkan replies that he often develops anger towards the teachers in class. He would then suddenly feel like hitting the adult. He couldn't name the cause, but if the teacher behaved unkindly towards him, he would have even greater problems holding back than if the teacher was nice to him.

The school management holds a preliminary meeting with the class teacher to inform them in advance about Serkan's problem. In a discussion with Serkan and the teacher, they look for a solution with the aim of ensuring Serkan's participation in class on the one hand and the teacher's safety on the other. They agree that if he gets angry with the teacher, he will attach a magnet to the blackboard and leave the room quietly. The magnet symbolises a time out. During the time out, which can last a maximum of 15 minutes, Serkan jogs three laps around the schoolyard, which he says helps him to reduce his anger. He then returns to class and takes part in lessons.

With this help, Serkan manages to graduate from school. The frequency of situations in which he has to resort to Time Out is becoming increasingly rare.

2.3.10 Trigger acoustic signal

Milan

Mrs Müller is supervising the break in the school playground. A group of young people from outside the school ask pupils about a boy called Milan (14). When they find out where he is, they circle him, clench their fists and the leader of the group says to Milan: "Now we're going to finish you off!" Mrs Müller tries to get the youngsters to stop. But they don't react to her. Other pupils see the conflict and want to help Milan. When the strangers attack Milan, Mrs Müller pulls a *shrill alarm* (manual trigger alarm) out of her bag and sets it off. The young people look around in horror, react with panic and scatter. The strangers then flee the school grounds.

In the subsequent conversation between Mrs Müller and Milan, he reports that the young people who tried to beat him up belong to a youth gang and suspect that he has a relationship with the girlfriend of the leader of the group. Milan knows which school the youths attend. Ms Müller suggests that Milan ask the school social work specialists at both schools to organise a meeting to resolve the conflict. Milan likes the suggestion. Mrs Müller discusses the incident with the school's social worker.

2.4 Reparation instead of punishment

Dmytro

The break is over. All the pupils go to their classrooms. Dmytro (16) has always been late for physics lessons over the last few weeks. Today he is determined to be on time. He can already see the physics teacher standing at the door of the classroom. Dmytro races towards the teacher, stops right in front of him and grins at him. The physics teacher is shocked. He thinks that Dmytro is going to run him down or hit him.

The physics teacher contacts the school management. She asks him what he needs in order to be able to continue working with the pupil. He says that he would like a class conference as he feels massively threatened by Dmytro's behaviour. In the class conference, Dmytro apologises to the physics teacher. It is decided that for the next four weeks, Dmytro will support the physics teacher with all his break-time supervision in the corridor outside the physics room. Dmytro takes on this task. The physics teacher is very happy with the solution. In addition, Dmytro is now always on time for his physics lessons.

This case study is an example of how important it is that children or young people who have made a mistake are given the opportunity to make amends. This is also illustrated by other case studies in this book: *Sanna* (see 2.3.3), *Muhammed* (see 3.2.6) and *Svea* (see 6.3). By making amends, the pupil's feelings of guilt and the teacher's offence can be resolved. Future encounters in class and during breaks are freed from negative feelings such as rejection and aggression. The older a pupil is, the more he or she must be given the opportunity to develop a solution themselves or with peers. Reparation as a possible solution to misbehaviour should be anchored in the class or school rules of every school (chapters 6.3 and 8).

2.5 Conclusion

In this chapter, the reasons for provocations and aggressive behaviour towards teachers were presented first. Three possibilities for educational action were presented on the basis of exehome officemplary case studies: the educational attitude, the *cut* to interrupt destructive processes and the principle of reparation instead of punishment.

To prevent conflicts, the educational attitude at the relationship level is of crucial importance. Appreciation, praise and recognition are principles in the organisation of educational interactions. Difficult educational situations often arise due to *negative transference* from pupils to teachers. It is then important to interrupt the situation in order to stop aggressive or violent behaviour.

Ten tools for creating a *cut* in conflict situations were presented in this chapter. The use of these tools ensures that teachers can adhere to the principles of appreciative educational behaviour as described in the *Reckahn Reflections on the Ethics of Educational Relationships* (Prengel 2017). The use of the tools presented to create a *cut* in difficult situations therefore serves to protect the pupil as well as the teacher's self-protection.

The tools for creating a *cut* should be part of the health management programme for teachers and should be taught in training courses when teachers join the teaching profession (Hehn-Oldiges 2021). This offer should be made in particular to teachers who, due to their subject combination, only teach learning groups for a small number of hours per school week.

To support the emotional and social development of pupils, it is very important that they are not punished after misbehaviour, because punishments tend to reinforce aggressive tendencies in the interaction between teachers and pupils rather than reduce them. Instead, it is important that the teacher offers the opportunity to make amends. In this way, they can make it clear that they mean well with the child or young person in order to build trust. All efforts by teachers or socio-educational professionals to shape their interactions with their pupils can be particularly effective if they are institutionally supported by the school policy and school rules (Chapter 6).

3. Pupils harm others

3.1 Theoretical considerations

At school, children learn and play in groups. In order for school to be a social place for pupils where they feel safe, there are rules for interacting with each other. Children and young people with challenging behaviour often find it difficult to cope in groups (Becker 2008, 2022; Oswald 2009). In the presence of classmates, they come under competitive pressure when it comes to getting the attention of teachers or older pupils, and they often feel provoked by others or called upon to intervene when other children or young people do not follow the rules.

The causes of behaviour that harms others or endangers classmates vary from person to person. Behaviour that harms others is often triggered unconsciously. Family constellations of the children often play a role, especially sibling constellations.

Children or young people with traumatic experiences are more likely to react intensely to the behaviour of their classmates than others. They allow themselves to be triggered. This can manifest itself in extreme withdrawal behaviour as well as aggressive behaviour that causes psychological harm or even physical injury to classmates. The triggers are often incomprehensible to teachers and are experienced as inappropriate. This is why it is important for the further development of the children and young people concerned to deal with each incident in regular team meetings. All those involved in the team can then find out what moves young people when they behave challengingly and develop constructive responses.

3.2 Solutions for conflicts in everyday school life

3.2.1 Reactivation of sibling conflicts

Moving up instead of staying down in school (Becker 2021a, 13-16)

Mirac

Mirac (8) started primary school three years ago. Mirac is being supported in a programme for neighbourhood-oriented multiple offenders. He has already been charged with 39 offences of robbery. Investigations have shown that his older brothers are instigating him to commit the offences. Apparently he is supposed to rob valuables from shops for them.

Mirac has just moved into a new flat with his single mother and his three older brothers. As the flat is in a different part of the city, the change of residence leads to a change of school and the responsibility of a different youth welfare office. As the family has already received several forms of educational support, each of which was terminated by the mother, Mirac is no longer the focus of the youth welfare office due to the change of residence. Mirac has already been expelled from two schools, so he is starting at a new school for the third time.

His mother has sole custody as his father is in prison for assault resulting in death. The family lost their last home because Mirac and his younger sister threw small pieces of furniture out of the window at night and listened to loud music while their mother and older brothers worked at night.

Mirac attends his new school, a community school, irregularly. He does not respond to the teachers when they speak to him. He runs around the room restlessly, sweeps the other children's work materials off the table, hits them in the face or punches them hard on the arm. When he takes up his own workstation, he takes a brief interest in the materials before putting his head down on the table and soon getting up again to run around the room. During breaks, he bullies his classmates without the teachers noticing or the children daring to talk about it. He uses threats of violence and physical violence if they do not comply (Becker 2021a, 13).

During an impromptu home visit, the class teacher meets the mother. Even in her presence, Mirac appears very restless and aggressive. On the other hand, he is calm and friendly around his older brothers. The home visit leads to a school support conference, which takes place two weeks later with the mother, a police officer who looks after Mirac and a representative of the youth welfare office. In this meeting, an attempt is made to find solutions that build on his strengths. Mirac seems to feel safe in the presence of his older brothers and can obviously concentrate on learning in their presence. His mother says that they have already done homework with him, which has worked very well. In general, Mirac is a quiet boy at home with his older brothers.

The idea was born to take up this positive experience with the big brothers and ask the tenth-grader if he could study there for a few weeks. The tenth-graders agree. Two mentors were found for Mirac and it was agreed that he would learn with learning materials from his year group in tenth grade. From the very first day, Mirac enjoys coming to tenth grade and is no longer absent. He is very calm and well-adjusted in this class. Mirac seems happy and well-balanced. The mentors explain tasks to him and support him. In addition, he receives one lesson a day from the class teacher of his home class, which serves to build relationships and teach him new learning content for his year group. After three months, Mirac gradually takes part in lessons in his year group. In the meantime, it was possible to organise his admission to a day group, a semi-residential placement in the afternoon. In addition, the mother was supported in a counselling process through regular short home visits, during which only Mirac's small daily successes were discussed. The mother agreed to the help, as the youth welfare office employee informed the mother that Mirac would otherwise be placed in an inpatient facility without her consent (Becker 2021a,14).

Mirac did not receive any support from his parents from an early age. Overall, Mirac grew up in an environment that did not allow him to develop a basic trust but rather a massive fear of destruction that controlled his behaviour at school from the unconscious. He fends off his anxieties and feelings of powerlessness through hyperactive and violent behaviour, which makes him feel strong (Becker 1995a, Erikson 2021, Winnicott 2023). The thefts on behalf of his older brothers provide him with positive attention and esteem, so that he can feel safe and secure with them (Becker 2021a, 15).

Individual table instead of group table

Justine

It's breakfast break in a class with inter-year lessons 1 to 3. Julia and Justine sit next to each other at a group table with a total of four girls. Conflicts often arise because Justine uses her elbows to push the other girls' objects so far back onto their half of the table that she has more space than everyone else. The other girls usually tolerate this, as Justine otherwise quickly reacts aggressively to them verbally and they want to avoid this. Today Julia takes out her lunch box and opens it. She starts shouting: "Mum put chocolate biscuits in my lunch box. Now they're gone. That was Justine again." Justine jumps up and wants to slap Julia. The teacher asks calmly: "Justine, where's your lunch box?" "I didn't get one from Mum. Night shift. You know what I mean. Julia always gets chocolate biscuits and I don't. I have to eat something too."

The class teacher makes a home visit. The mother says that she has to sleep in in the morning as she often works nights. She reports about Justine that she was already categorised as a child with support needs at the daycare centre and received support.

Justine has two older and three younger siblings. There are fewer beds in the children's room than there are children. In the kitchen, there is one less chair at the dining table than there are people in the household. The food that is brought to the table at mealtimes is often not enough for everyone. At home, Justine has to fight for a place at the dining table with her elbows. When she succeeds in doing this in front of her brothers, she is praised by her mother.

Justine behaves in class as she does at home. She behaves in the same way that she does at home. Justine doesn't realise that she doesn't have to fight for her place at the group table. The class teacher has allocated Justine a place at the group table with four girls to ensure her social participation in the class.

It was only in a case consultation that took place after the home visit that the class teacher realised that Justine did not have her own seat in her family's home. She has her own seat at the group table, but it is so close to the seats of her classmates that she cannot recognise it as her own. Instead, the situation at home is unconsciously reactivated and she fights for her place at the group table and for the teacher's attention, just like at home. She recognises Justine's problem. She suggests that Justine sit at an individual table near the teacher's table. Justine is happy about this suggestion and feels valued by the teacher. This individual seat gives her so much security that she can learn well here and from this table she can approach her classmates, who were previously sitting with her at the group table, for joint play or learning activities and play or learn with them without conflict.

At the same time, the teacher liaises with the family support worker. Together with the mother, they work out that Justine should have her own bed at home, enough food and her own chair at the dining table. The mother recognises her daughter's need and provides both. She also receives support in providing the children with food. As the mother is unable to get up in the morning to prepare the school breakfast for her children, even with support, the following solution is found at school:

Justine receives breakfast and a lunch box with breakfast before lessons in the school's all-day area.

This case study shows that social participation in playing and learning in groups can sometimes be made possible by a solution that initially appears to be segregation. As in Justine's case, it is therefore crucial to understand the individual causes of a child's behaviour.

Valuing older children in mixed-age classes

Kevin

Kevin is the eldest of four siblings. All four children are growing up with their father. The mother currently has no right of access due to serious mental health problems. The father told the children from an early age that their mother had abandoned them. All of the children show attachment disorders and behaviour at daycare and later at school that is described by teachers as very challenging.

The father wants his sons to become football stars. Kevin proves to be clumsy at ball games, while the younger children love playing football with their father and have a lot of fun. The father also reports that he wants to bring up his children strictly. The teachers suspect that the father beats his children. However, they have never been able to find any physical signs of violence in Kevin or his younger siblings. They regularly raise the issue of violence towards the children in conversations with the father. He states that he strictly rejects violence towards children. In addition to his wish for his children to become football stars, a good school-leaving certificate for his children is very important to him.

As a sixth-grader in the mixed-age group of years four to six, Kevin demonstrates the following behaviour: He takes the class rules very seriously and makes sure that the other pupils adhere to them. He does this especially with the younger pupils. When rules are broken, he physically stands next to the younger children and shouts at them so that they behave in accordance with the rules immediately. The teachers observe this critically, but let him get away with it. They don't talk to him about it at first. After a while, they notice that Kevin summons children who break a rule for the second time into the classroom, takes his belt out of his trousers and hits them with it.

In subsequent conversations it turns out that he helps his father at home with the upbringing of his younger siblings and of course he would also support the teachers in the classroom with the upbringing of the younger children.

In a case consultation in which the teachers of the class participate, it becomes clear that Kevin takes on this task at home in identification with his father but also to receive appreciation and praise from his father. This is particularly important to him as he is clumsy when playing football.

The teachers realise that, like the father, they have hardly paid any attention to Kevin so far. Instead, the younger children in the mixed-age class were at the centre of their attention. From now on, they praise Kevin because he takes care to follow the rules. They teach him how this can be done in an appreciative manner and that hitting or other forms of violence are forbidden.

From now on, the class teacher will have a feedback meeting with Kevin twice a week. The day, time and location of the meeting will be specified. The topic is also put on the agenda of the class council. There, they work out how Kevin can draw others' attention to rule violations in an appreciative manner and remind them of the rule. The class council decides that not only Kevin should take on this task, but that this should be done by all pupils in turn. In the first week, it is Kevin's turn. In each school week, only one class rule should be observed. In the first week, the rule is as follows: "I throw rubbish in one of the rubbish bins provided for waste separation." Every child in the class has a magnet with their name on it. From now on, these should always hang on the blackboard in a green field. A red box is drawn next to it. If rules are broken, Kevin hangs the child's magnet in the red box. At the end of the lesson, the teacher asks the children whose magnet is in the red box to stay in the room and pick up the rubbish lying on the floor and throw it in the appropriate rubbish bin.

The class council regularly discusses how to deal with rule violations. The topic is no longer just Kevin's concern, but has become a concern for the class. Kevin also suggests that the other sixth-formers who are committed to upholding the rules should also take part in the two weekly feedback meetings. This suggestion is accepted by the class teacher and from now on the sixth-formers can act as learning locomotives for the younger pupils in this area.

The cases of reactivation of sibling conflicts at school presented here show how conflicts can arise in learning groups as a result of sibling rivalries. At the same time, understanding sibling constellations opens up a large reservoir of possible solutions for conflicts between pupils.

Children unconsciously reactivate their relationships with their siblings at school. Pupils often behave towards each other as they would towards their brothers and sisters, which can threaten and endanger classmates if their behaviour is aggressive. If a child experiences that only the younger children in the family receive praise and attention from their parents, it is possible that the anger towards the younger siblings is unconsciously reactivated towards younger children in the mixed-grade class.

Temporarily attending a higher year group is an effective measure that should be clarified here once again. As in the case of *Mirac* (see 3.2.1), moving to a different class can change the position of the child concerned in the learning group in such a way that it can have a miraculous effect in terms of social participation. Temporary attendance at a higher class level does not require any staff resources and can be organised quickly with little effort. It is important to actively involve the teachers of the receiving class, the pupil concerned and the parents in the planning process.

The solution should only be implemented with the parents' consent and set out in a joint agreement. So far, parents have never rejected this solution, as they do not see the temporary attendance of a higher year group as devaluation or segregation.

Attendance at a higher year group should be limited in terms of the number of hours per week and school weeks. An appointment for an evaluation meeting should be arranged with the parents and the child or young person at the planning stage. It is of central importance for the positive development of the children and young people that they learn from the work plans of their year group and that the temporary visit takes place in a year group in which the pupils are at least two years older.

3.2.2 Neglect

Marcel

Marcel (8) is in his third year of the flexible school entry phase. He has difficulties with counting and visualising quantities. The teachers know from his parents that he has three siblings.
But he always talks about six children in the family.

Marcel also attracts the attention of teachers because he generally enters the classroom very loudly or likes to play *dog when* he comes in the door. He then moves on all fours and sneaks past the teachers' legs before sitting down next to their feet. Sometimes he also imitates the barking of a dog.

During the home visit and in a joint case consultation with the family support worker, it becomes clear that the parents have two dogs with whom they spend many hours a day sitting on the sofa in front of the television. They cuddle the dogs. They also walk the dogs several times a day and worry about their diet. Apparently the parents don't react to Marcel coming home. He learns that the dogs receive love and attention from his parents and that they only react to him when he comes banging and shouting in the door. Then the parents shout: "Now shut up. Go to your room. We're watching telly!" He must get the impression that the pets are preferred to him and his siblings and are at least equal to the children. Marcel pretends to be a dog at school because he unconsciously hopes for attention from the teachers. Entering the classroom loudly serves the same purpose.

Understanding the relationship constellations in Marcel's family also explains why he speaks of five siblings instead of three. He has added the two dogs to the siblings. This is confirmed when he is asked to give the names of the siblings and also mentions the dogs' names as a matter of course.

Outreach family therapy is key to solving Marcel's difficulties. To accompany this, Marcel can be offered learning therapy programmes at school and it can be suggested in discussions that he is allowed to play *dog* with other children throughout the day and during breaks. In class, he should learn as Marcel.

Teachers endeavour to greet him by name at the start of the lesson, to frequently call on him in class when answering questions or solving problems and to always address him by name. In maths lessons, he is first given playful and then written maths problems to form classifications, so that he increasingly learns to form generic terms and subgroups and to operate mathematically with them. For example, he learns that apples and pears are types of fruit, but that the purchase price has to be calculated differently.

Provocations - add fuel to the fire

René

René (13) has an identified special educational need in the area of emotional and social development. He is a year 8 pupil at a comprehensive school. René has problems putting his work materials on the desk on time at the beginning of his Russian lesson. When he is approached by the teacher, he often sweeps his pencil case and folder off the table, throws paper balls at his classmates or starts running games with them.

The teachers have already tried to help René organise his work with reinforcement programmes. Unfortunately without success. In a one-to-one discussion between the school social work specialist and René, it emerges that his classmates at René's group table are apparently encouraging him to delay the start of lessons by disrupting them in a way that is familiar to the teachers. René, who feels that this earns him the appreciation of his classmates, regularly agrees to this.

The school social worker has a conversation with René and his table group to talk to them about the negative consequences for René. His performance in Russian will probably be graded as unsatisfactory in his next report, which will have consequences for his school career. It turns out that they don't want to harm René in any way. On the contrary, they want to support him from now on. René and his classmates agree with the school social worker that they can go on an excursion of their choice on a school day if René's performance in Russian is graded as sufficient on his next report card. In a conversation with René, they discuss who can support him and how. From now on, they help René to have the work materials ready at the start of lessons and to work well. Among other things, they meet up to practise vocabulary for vocabulary tests together.

To the surprise of the Russian teacher, René's working behaviour and performance change very quickly. The influence of the table group is decisive for his learning success and his working behaviour. In retrospect, it becomes clear that his classmates themselves had an interest in delaying the start of the lesson and disrupting it. The young people knew that they were only adding *fuel to the fire* because of his individual problems. After realising that they were putting his school career at risk by doing so, they now support René, which contributes to his immediate learning success.

3.2.3 Bullying

Amy, Liz and Ronja

Amy is 15 years old. She suffers from diagnosed anorexia and shows borderline symptoms. After a stay in hospital, she is on the road to recovery and attends the ninth grade of a grammar school. When she meets up with her classmates, they often take photos of each other or film themselves dancing with their smartphones. Ronja, one of Amy's classmates, accidentally comes across pictures of her best friend Liz posted on Snapchat. The photos are a series of photos that Amy has taken of Liz. The girl can be seen dressed revealingly, naked, wearing make-up, without make-up or making sexually suggestive gestures. The sentence "I'm going to puke!" is added to each photo. Ronja tells Liz about the photos. Liz is very ashamed of the photos, suddenly hates herself and fears that many of her classmates may have seen them. She locks herself in her room, cries and doesn't want to go to school any more.

Ronja tells the teacher about the incident. The teacher, Mrs Meyer, is upset and feels the need to punish Amy. However, due to Amy's illness, she also wants to treat her gently to prevent a relapse. As the photos were only posted on Snapchat for a short time and were apparently only seen by Ronja in class, it cannot be proven that Amy was the one who uploaded the photos. In a conversation with the teacher, Amy initially denies this and claims that Liz could have uploaded the photos herself.

Liz returns to school when she learns from Ronja and the teacher that apparently no one but Ronja has seen the photos of Liz. In a case consultation with the teachers working in the classroom, which is moderated by the school psychologist, it becomes clear that as a result of the incident described, Liz is displaying symptoms that Amy had previously shown. By posting the photos with the sentence "I'm going to puke!", Amy presumably manages to relieve herself of her own feelings of inadequacy and self-hatred. Amy feels stronger as a result. Liz unconsciously identifies with this and withdraws, ashamed and full of self-hatred. In the case consultation, it is decided to involve Amy's therapist, who discusses the incident with her. Afterwards, Amy appears visibly affected by the damage she has caused Liz. In the next step, the teacher discusses with Amy, Liz and Ronja what could be done to make up for the damage done to Liz. The teacher suggests that Amy, Liz and Ronja set up a group for the school class on a messenger service, which the three girls should supervise with a view to communicating only in a respectful way about other people.

3.2.4 Stigmatisation

Ibrahim

Selin (15) is in tenth grade at a secondary school. Around 40 per cent of the pupils in her class are Muslim. Some of the girls wear a headscarf. Selin took off her headscarf a fortnight ago. Since then, her classmate Ibrahim has regularly called her a slut. This happens when he meets her alone. Ibrahim has special educational needs in the area of mental development. Selin therefore thinks that he cannot control his behaviour due to his impairment. He is annoying, but you just have to put up with it and not worry about it. She tells her friends, who advise her to inform the class teacher. In the end, they decide to go and see the teacher together. The class teacher, Mr Müller, tries to talk to Ibrahim. Ibrahim does not agree and refers to his parents, who allegedly also believe that girls should wear a headscarf. Mr Müller invites the parents and Ibrahim to talk to him. The parents are appalled by Ibrahim's behaviour. They tell him in the presence of the teacher that they would not tolerate this behaviour towards a girl. They want him to apologise to Selin. When Ibrahim realises that his parents and Mr Müller are of the same opinion, his attitude changes. He says he is sorry. Mr Müller asks if he has any idea how he can make amends for his behaviour. Ibrahim suggests apologising to Selin in front of the class and giving her a flower. This will take place the following morning in the class council.

3.2.5 Discrimination because of clan family names

Samir

Samir (13) is in seventh grade at a community school. Samir has an identified need for learning support. Recently, he has been shunned by his classmates. They refuse any contact to play football or table tennis during the breaks in a friendly manner. Samir reacts aggressively to this rejection. He bumps into them or hits them on the shoulder from behind as they walk past. His classmates find this behaviour very unpleasant and bring it up in the class council.

In the class council, it turns out that nobody wants anything more to do with Samir. Samir has a surname that is known in Berlin as the surname of a so-called clan family that originally comes from Lebanon. During the summer holidays, a man with this surname was killed. It turns out that the pupils are afraid of also becoming victims of violence. They want nothing to do with Samir or his family so as not to expose themselves to this danger.

The teacher, who has only been working at the school for a few weeks, enquires about the murder and contacts the police prevention officer. It turns out that Samir is not related to the person who was killed and that his family has nothing to do with the victim's family. The teacher invites the prevention officer into the classroom. He can answer all the young people's questions and allay their fears about the dangers posed by Samir's family. The pupils actively approach Samir and arrange to meet him again regularly to play football or table tennis. He is invited to birthday parties again. In retrospect, it is clear that his behaviour, which was described by the young people in the class council as stressful, was caused by the experience of suddenly being ostracised and shunned. He was discriminated against because of his surname.

3.2.6 Non-compliance with rules of faith

Muhammed

It is Ramadan. Most of the pupils at a comprehensive school in the Ruhr region are Christian or do not belong to any religious community. Around a third of the pupils are Muslim. All young people of Muslim faith at this school take part in the fasting month of Ramadan. During these weeks, they abstain from food and drink from sunrise to sunset. Smoking is also prohibited. The month of fasting lasts 30 days and ends with a three-day festival, Eid.

At the same time as Ramadan, important class tests are being written at school. Fatih really wants to do well so that he can transfer to grammar school. That's why the grades he gets in these tests are important to him. Fatih wants to study medicine after leaving school. Fatih decides not to take part in Ramadan because of the class tests.

Muhammed, a 15-year-old pupil in Year 9 who attends a Koranic school at the weekend, happens to be in the school playground when Fatih leaves the school building thirty minutes after school finishes. Muhammed insults him, hits him and spits at him because Fatih, as a Muslim, is not taking part in Ramadan. Fatih is shocked by this attack, but manages to get away from Muhammed and reports the incident to his class teacher.

Muhammed has special educational needs in the area of emotional and social development. He stands out because he either ignores school rules or is particularly strict about adhering to them. Muhammed has not yet been able to develop a tolerance for ambiguity. The teacher discusses the incident with the school social work specialist and the school management.

This incident is a physical assault in connection with a religious affiliation. The school management files a criminal complaint and invites the pupils to a class conference. The school management speaks to Muhammed and his parents the next morning. The class teacher informs the class about the incident. It turns out that the Muslim pupils admire Muhammed's behaviour. Not taking part in Ramadan is forbidden. It becomes clear that Muhammed has picked up on the negative sentiment towards Fatih and, when he met him by chance in the school playground, turned it into an action. The pupils react emotionally. The teacher can reconstruct the events with the class.

The incident is taken as an opportunity to invite an imam to the class. Parents and young people take part in the discussion with the imam. The imam explains which groups of people should participate in Ramadan according to the Koran. To the surprise of the parents and young people, it turns out that Ramadan can be suspended for important exams and made up for later, for example during the summer holidays. The pupils of the Muslim faith realise that Fatih can not only decide for himself whether he wants to participate in Ramadan, but that he is also acting as a good Muslim according to the Koran if he does not participate in Ramadan during the exams.

The young people in the class realise that they have triggered Muhammad's behaviour with their comments. In retrospect, they are sorry for this. In a class conference, the pupils, parents and teachers involved decide that Muhammed must make amends. He should apologise to Fatih and, together with three other pupils, go to all the classes in the school and give a short talk about Ramadan to inform all the young people about the rules and prevent further incidents. Fatih is free to decide whether he wants to take part in these short presentations. He decides in favour. The school management informs the police about the reparation, which has a positive effect on the handling of the criminal charges.

3.3 Conclusion

The causes of behaviour that harms others or endangers classmates vary from person to person. In the case of children or young people who display challenging behaviour, the causes are often seen in a mental illness. Only an understanding of the subjective processing of experiences in the family or at school can help to find the individual reasons for challenging behaviour. It becomes clear that behaviour that harms others is sometimes triggered unconsciously. Family constellations, especially sibling constellations, religious affiliation or the child's culture of origin can play a decisive role here. Classmates, parents or teachers can facilitate or even trigger the initiation or consolidation of aggressive behaviour. The most effective educational interventions should be sought and found through co-operation within the multi-professional team, the participation of the affected pupils and the class community.

4. Pupils harm themselves

4.1 Theoretical considerations

In almost all cases, self-harming behaviour in the classroom can be attributed to two sets of causes:
- For pupils with intellectual disabilities or an autism spectrum disorder, the cause may be overstimulation if the teaching programmes have not yet been tailored to a pupil's needs (Theunissen/Kulig 2015).
- Children or adolescents with impaired emotional development who have experienced too little support in early childhood or have had traumatic experiences sometimes endanger themselves or develop auto-aggressive behaviour (Auchter 1994, Becker 1995a, Winnicott 2023).

In most cases, affected children and adolescents are presented to child and adolescent psychiatric practices or clinics and there is a need for psychotherapeutic treatment. A need for educational support is also frequently identified. This chapter aims to show which educational measures are useful to enable participation in inclusive education. The causes of auto-aggressive behaviour vary from individual to individual and can be identified by understanding the case during supervision or case counselling. This is important in order to be able to plan and implement tailored educational programmes. In principle, self-harming behaviour can arise in children and young people with mental health problems for the following reasons:
- The aggression they develop towards others is directed towards themselves (e.g. hitting or hurting themselves).
- They aggressively fend off fears or depressive feelings. In turn, they turn this aggression against themselves. This enables them to feel themselves better (e.g. by scratching).
- They unconsciously identify with the depressive feelings of their parents or friends. The pupil acts out their feelings on their behalf (Günther/Bruns 2010).

4.2 Solutions for conflicts in everyday school life

4.2.1 Sensory overload

Tom

Tom (7) starts primary school close to home. As a child with intellectual disabilities, he previously attended a children's centre with ten children. There was close co-operation with the parents. This collaboration included daily conversations at morning drop-off and pick-up.

Tom joins a primary school class of 23 children. He is very restless from day one. Before he started school, a handover meeting was held with the nursery school teachers. In addition to the primary school teacher, a special needs teacher works eight hours a week in the classroom and an integration assistant works twelve hours a week. As in the Kinderladen, there are morning meetings and an exchange between one of the parents/guardians and the class teacher at pick-up.

Tom shows pronounced auto-aggressive behaviour right from the start. He bites his wrists, runs around the classroom, opens the windows and wants to climb through the window from the second floor into the courtyard. The windows are locked by the teachers so that they can no longer be opened, whereupon he leaves the classroom and no longer responds to the teachers. From the third day onwards, he dozes off every day at around 12.00 noon. From the fourth day onwards, he runs around the whole school building and onto the street. The teachers are desperate as all efforts to integrate him into the classroom community fail.

At the end of the full-day lessons, Tom lies down on a mat and sleeps for a long time. He then eats with a small group of children at a group table in the all-day room. Afterwards, he plays alone with cars on the play mat and seems content.

The teachers begin to teach him one-to-one in a small adjoining room for four hours a day. This works well, and the symptoms of running away and defecating disappear. After three weeks, they teach him alone in the first two lessons and in the third and fourth lessons, other children from the class are brought into the adjoining room to learn maths with him. After five weeks, Tom takes part in the morning circle in class.

In retrospect, the causes of Tom's behaviour in the classroom are discussed in a collegial case consultation. On the one hand, the many children and activities cause him anxieties and act as a sensory overload. Secondly, he is not given enough quiet time in the classroom. Instead, Tom is given learning tasks that are geared towards his level of development, but which are given to him too close together in terms of time. In addition, although the tasks are much easier than those of his classmates, they are too cognitively orientated overall.

Tom primarily needs practical tasks that are placed in a socially meaningful context within the class community.

After the team recognised that Tom was overwhelmed, the teachers' attitude changed. They plan more rest breaks and practical tasks into his daily schedule, so that after twelve weeks he can spend most of his time learning in the classroom and only works for two hours a day with a few other children in the next room.

4.2.2 Separation anxiety

Alina

Alina (7) and her mother arrived in Berlin six weeks ago after fleeing from Ukraine. Alina is enrolled at the local primary school to attend second grade and is taken to school on the first day. There, however, the girl refuses to be separated from her mother and let her leave. Alina begins to cry and clings to her mother. Over the course of several weeks, her mother stays in class for the first two lessons in the morning. But whenever she wants to leave the classroom, the behaviour described is repeated.

The teachers advise the mum to simply leave the room. They would look after Alina and presumably she would calm down after a short time and play or learn with the other children. When the mother leaves the classroom, Alina immediately kicks her chair, screams, bites herself and pulls her own hair until she is injured. The mother hears Alina's screams from outside and returns to the classroom. As her mother has to work from home, she has no choice but to go home with Alina. At home, Alina keeps herself busy and her mother can work in peace.

The teachers observe Alina's remarkably close relationship with her mother. They call in the school psychology service. During the anamnesis interview, the school psychologist learns that Alina's mother separated from her father three and a half years ago and moved to another city with Alina. Neither of them knew anyone there. When the mother had to be taken to hospital because of a ruptured appendix, Alina was placed in a home for the duration of her mother's hospitalisation. According to the mother's account, she was told that Alina had behaved well there. She was very quiet and passive, which is why the carers at the home were worried. After her mother's return from hospital, Alina maintained her very quiet behaviour, which the mother noticed but had not yet found worrying.

In the further course of the discussions with the school psychologist, the mother understands that when Alina attends school, she unconsciously reactivates the separation experiences and separation anxiety that she experienced during her mother's hospitalisation. As there were no attachment figures for Alina when her mother was hospitalised, she experienced the separation as traumatic. Alina probably felt abandoned and rejected by the sudden disappearance of her mother, who was suddenly hospitalised.

When she started school, these experiences were reactivated, so that when Alina went to school she reacted as if she was being abandoned forever. Her clinging to her mother and refusal to let her go is the result of strong separation anxiety. The mother was also unable to leave Alina at school, although she realised that the teachers were taking very good care of Alina's well-being.

The case presented here clearly illustrates how a mother-child relationship that is too close can hinder a child's development. The symbiotic fusion between the two leads to massive separation anxiety in both mother and child. As a result of the traumatic experience of separation at kindergarten age, the relationship between closeness and distance is so out of balance that neither can leave the other without experiencing the fear of being separated from the other forever. The realisation of the cause of Alina and her mother's separation anxiety led to a change in attitude among the teachers. With the support of externally moderated case counselling, it is possible to find a solution:

A teacher who works in all-day care for the class works with Alina and her mother to develop a way that allows Alina to let her mother go. The amount of time her mother leaves the room and then the school is tailored to Alina's fears. Alina's smartphone is used to enable her mother and Alina to be temporarily separated during the course of the day. It is agreed that if Alina thinks she needs to see her mum immediately to reassure her, she will type an animal symbol into her smartphone and send it to her. The mum undertakes to respond with the same animal symbol as soon as possible. Alina's detachment from her mother can be achieved in four phases:

- Phase 1: The mother leaves the classroom and stays in the corridor.
- Phase 2: She goes home and comes back two hours later.
- Phase 3: The mum picks Alina up after class and accompanies her and the class to the school canteen for lunch.
- Phase 4: Alina is taken to school by her mum in the morning and picks her up again at 4.00 pm.

In all four phases, communication via smartphone (see above) can be used as soon as Alina feels insecure or anxious. During phases 1 and 2, the mother finds it difficult to accept that Alina no longer needs her. The school psychologist refers the mother to a parenting counsellor who offers weekly sessions to discuss her separation anxietiy and its causes. Alina manages to attend school regularly and feels increasingly comfortable in class, so that after three months she can even go to school on her own in the mornings.

As a result of the educational counselling, the symbiotic relationship between mother and daughter gradually dissolves. The mother's job and Alina's school attendance are the decisive prerequisites for this.

4.2.3 Self-harming behaviour such as scratching

Tara

Tara (15) is in tenth grade at a secondary school. She has already been hospitalised in a psychiatric ward several times. There she was diagnosed with more than two years of school underachievement and anxieties as a result of prolonged experiences of failure. After her hospitalisation, she unsuccessfully completed her probationary period in a practical class and returned to her secondary school. She is very often late in her class and never completes her homework. She gets into verbally aggressive arguments in the school playground. Her school performance in German and maths is in line with the framework curriculum for year six. She is good with a calculator and can read very well.

Tara has long dyed blonde hair, long black eyelashes glued on, is heavily made up and dressed in strikingly fashionable clothes. From a distance, she appears very self-confident. As soon as she is approached by a teacher, she answers with a trembling voice and proves to be very anxious, which is in extreme contrast to her outward appearance. Tara quickly gains confidence when you talk to her like a child.

Tara does not tolerate criticism: as soon as her unfinished homework, her daily lateness or her unauthorised smoking on the school grounds are addressed, she feels threatened, which is expressed in a radical change in her voice. Suddenly her voice no longer seems insecure, but loud and aggressive: "Why are you bringing this up now? This has nothing to do with your subject. That's not fair!" Tara then gets up, runs to the toilet, locks herself in and slashes her arms with a razor blade. Questions arise: What could be the causes of the scratching? What solutions are there for organising everyday school life with Tara?

Solution for organising everyday school life with Tara

After discussions between the school social worker, her father, Tara, and the caseworker from the youth welfare office, Tara begins psychotherapy, which was already recommended to her during her stay at the child and adolescent psychiatric centre. In psychotherapy, she is able to learn to understand her experiences of separation in early childhood as the cause of her behaviour and attend school more regularly as the therapy progresses.

Within the school, the team decides that the school social worker should be available to her as her main point of contact. Tara meets with her every day during the big break to have breakfast together and talk about her worries if necessary. In addition, all teachers can call in the school social worker if Tara finds herself in situations where she needs support. It is crucial that Tara does not receive the social attention of adults and classmates when she scratches herself, but instead receives it through regular discussions with the school social worker, in the class council and in feedback discussions with the teacher and during peer-to-peer feedback in class.

The team of teachers has also agreed that Tara will no longer be spontaneously confronted in the school playground or corridor about missing homework, unauthorised smoking or being late. This only takes place in the discussions arranged with Tara, which are conducted in a solution- and resource-orientated manner. After the teachers were able to understand in supervision that scratching serves to prevent suicide, they react less strongly to this behaviour with fear. This new attitude on the part of the adults supports the success of the psychotherapy and the work of the school social worker. With the educational setting developed for Tara, regular school attendance is successful. In addition, Tara regularly makes small progress in German and maths.

The importance of scratching

Girls who scratch have usually experienced violence or deprivation, which characterises their current life (Heinemann/Hopf 2021). In adolescents, scratching serves as a defence against depressive feelings and as a suicide prophylaxis (Heinemann/Hopf 2021). Sachsse speaks of self-harm as self-care (Sachsse, 1987, p. 51). "The mastery of pain gives feelings of pride, strength and self-sufficiency, i.e. narcissistic gain" (Heinemann/Hopf 2021, 139) [translated by the author]. "I bleed, therefore I am" is the title of an essay by Kristin Teubert (1997), focussing on the emotional distress that girls experience when they scratch themselves.

"The girls who hurt themselves look at their bodies predominantly as if they were an external object that has become alien to them. When scratching, the body becomes a field of activity and they act on it as if it were inanimate. If they understood their body as the basis of life and sensation, they would not be able to act against it in this way. Just as they torture the body and soul themselves now, other people have done so in the past. The body becomes the object of aggression and thus replaces the you against whom the aggression should actually be directed" (Teubert 1997, 13) [translated by the author].

"Before and during the scratching, the young women are in a state of self-alienation (…) Their own bodies become alien to them, in their actions they are not aware of their ego. They are no longer sure of their existence, feelings can no longer be perceived or named. They no longer feel themselves and feel detached from everything, the world around them seems to sink into a fog. Everything becomes unreal, including themselves. This extremely frightening state (…) must be countered with something. Passively, they feel at the mercy of an urge or a force that causes them to cut themselves. By cutting themselves, the girls (…) bring themselves back to reality, they get closer to themselves and their environment again. They prove to themselves that they are still there, because now they can feel themselves. The pain that slowly sets in is a clear feeling that clearly belongs to them (Sachsse 1987, 51)" (Teubert 1997, 8ff.) [translated by the author].

Due to the narcissistic gain through scratching, the process of working with girls who scratch is a lengthy one, as initially educational action cannot offer an adequate substitute for self-harm (Teubert 1997). Scribing triggers incomprehension, anger, fear, pity or care in the adult counterpart (Heinemann/Hopf 2021). It is important that teachers and other educators learn to understand the individual emotional distress of a girl, preferably as a team in case supervision or counselling. It is also important to include the social context in which a girl lives. Understanding is the prerequisite for a sustainable educational relationship.

4.2.4 Hyperactivity

Timo

Timo (11) is in sixth grade at a primary school in Berlin. He regularly takes Ritalin to treat the attention deficit hyperactivity disorder (ADHD) (Becker 2006). In individual situations, Timo can concentrate very well on lesson content and perform well at school. Class tests that he writes in individual situations are usually graded well.

In class with 27 pupils, he sits at a single table because he attacks his table neighbours with pens, is constantly looking for his work materials and often accuses his table neighbours of stealing them. In the fifth or sixth lesson of a teaching day, such disputes often end in a fight in class. When doing written work in class, Timo fidgets restlessly in his chair and sometimes can't get a complete sentence onto his worksheet in a lesson. His performance in the classroom and in individual situations varies widely. The teachers believe that his concentration improves significantly when he takes the medication. At the same time, he often seems tired and sad. He repeatedly says that he wants to jump out of the third floor window because life has no meaning for him anyway. The school social worker looks after Timo. In a conversation with his parents or guardians, it emerges that Timo has not been hungry for several months and hardly eats anything. He goes to school in the morning without breakfast.

The child and adolescent psychiatry practice suggested psychotherapy for Timo. However, as his condition had initially improved with Ritalin, the parents saw no need to apply for psychotherapy. The parents only go to the doctor regularly to have Timo examined and to pick up a prescription for the Ritalin. The parents report to the paediatric psychiatrist that Timo is doing well on Ritalin.

A meeting of the student support group is held at the school, which is attended by the parents/guardians, a psychologist from the practice, the teachers, the school social worker and the caseworker from the youth welfare office. Agreements are made in this multi-professional discussion group:
- Timo's parents have breakfast with him at home in the morning before he goes to school.
- All teachers make sure that he takes part in the school lunch.
- Because Timo says he no longer wants to live, the parents now apply for the psychotherapy recommended by the doctor.

4.2.5 Individual retreat

Fatiya

Fatiya (7) is in her second year at an inclusive primary school. She has a 14-year-old sister and a 17-year-old brother. Both parents came to Germany as political refugees from Syria and have experienced torture.

Fatiya is overweight, appears apathetic, avoids movement, shows gross and fine motor abnormalities and visual perception disorders. She often cries when there is a lot of noise in class. Fatiya often feels ostracised by her classmates: "They won't let me play." Her classmates perceive Fatiya's mother as threatening and hide when she enters the school building. The school doctor recommended a paediatric psychiatric examination. An intelligence test was carried out and she was diagnosed with cognitive performance in the area of mental disability.

In the classroom, Fatiya looks like a big immovable boulder. If you talk to her calmly and with plenty of time, she can express herself reflectively on various topics. She worries a lot about her parents. This casts great doubt on the diagnosis of an intellectual disability.

The school social workers work very intensively with the parents. In light of their experiences in Syria, they have massive reservations about telling helpers from state institutions about their experiences and fears. This is why they have not taken advantage of counselling and therapy services so far. The parents are increasingly gaining trust through the parental counselling at the school. Gradually, it is possible to convince them of the need for psychotherapy to come to terms with their traumatic experiences in Syria and on the run. After a long wait, the treatment centre for victims of torture in Berlin offers them a place in therapy. As the parents' therapy progresses, Fatiya becomes more mobile at school. She begins to be motorically active, rarely cries and can increasingly learn independently within a temporary learning group. She is able to make rapid, significant progress in all subjects except maths. In fourth grade, she wins a class reading competition. Although she performs poorly in maths, she also improves in this subject to such an extent that she can transfer to secondary school after year six without special educational needs. In retrospect, it is clear that Fatiya was identified with her parents' fears (Becker/Prengel 2016b) and that this led to an emotionally induced learning and developmental blockade, which was mistaken for an intellectual disability.

4.2.6 Blows to your own body

Anton

Anton (6) grows up with his sister and brother with his father. His mother left the family when Anton was only a few months old. The youth welfare office then took custody away from her because Anton was beaten by her when he cried. The father works and manages to organise everyday life well with all three children. He makes sure that his children stick to the rules, behave politely and co-operate well in class.

Anton is in first grade, his younger siblings still go to daycare. Anton behaves quietly in class and is very well-adjusted. He has a prince-like beauty, often shines and is often chosen as a playmate, especially by girls. He receives a lot of attention from the teachers. During breaks and throughout the day, he often flouts the rules and provokes the teachers working there. They set age-appropriate boundaries for him, which leads to him retreating to the quiet room, becoming unresponsive, then taking off his socks, stuffing them in his mouth and hitting himself with his hands. The blows are so loud that they can be heard in the neighbouring room. The teachers develop great fears that he could hurt himself or hit them or other children. They are helpless and do not know how to stop the auto-aggressive behaviour.

When the nursery teachers tell the father about this, he doesn't believe them at first. These scenes are repeated up to three times a day and then don't appear at all for several weeks. The father suggests that the teachers film his son once. The teachers show him the film before deleting it again, whereupon he turns to the responsible social worker at the youth welfare office and asks for help. Anton first receives paediatric psychiatric and then psychotherapeutic help. The psychotherapist and the teachers at the school and the father work closely together. Understanding Anton's emotional situation means that his behaviour can be understood as a *dissociative phenomenon* and the situation can be dealt with professionally (Becker 2023, Urban 2021, 8-12).

Anton unconsciously transfers aspects of his primary caregiver, his mother, to the teachers in the all-day programme. In this context, the fears of destruction that he has developed towards his mother are reactivated. Due to the early loss of his mother, Anton developed an early childhood attachment disorder. His relationship with his father partially compensated for this. However, he only has a low frustration tolerance. Due to his father's strict upbringing, he does not show his aggression towards his teachers, but turns it against himself. As he wants to behave correctly, as expected by his father, he denies in retrospect that he hit himself and can no longer remember doing so.

A moderated case consultation is held with the entire team of teachers who teach or supervise Anton's learning group throughout the day. This enables everyone to understand Anton's behaviour and they are no longer afraid of him. It is very important for Anton that the teachers reduce their fears, as the adults' fears reinforce his own. In addition, an educator from the all-day programme is given hours to provide Anton with individual support. Among other things, she takes on ego functions as a educational specialist (Balint 1969, Geyer 2004). "On the one hand, interaction-related ego functions must be supplemented (…). On the other hand, the helping ego function must be realised in the form of a responding counterpart who makes his or her experience available to the patient, which also includes the role of the delimiting other (…)" (Geyer 2004, 328) [translated by the author]. The assumption of helping ego functions also includes regulating the balance between closeness and distance in the educational relationship. On this basis, a sustainable educational relationship develops between her and Anton. The teacher is in dialogue with him, shows him appreciation and praises him frequently, so that he experiences himself as self-effective. In conjunction with the psychotherapeutic treatment, this means that Anton is less likely to be overwhelmed by his anxieties and aggression and the scenes described above only occur occasionally. It is discussed with the educational team that in such situations, all objects that could hurt him are removed and the teacher present tries to talk to him in order to bring him back to reality. Anton is given a school companion to support him in everyday life during the whole day.

4.3 Conclusion

In the case of children or adolescents who endanger or harm themselves due to traumatic experiences or attachment disorders, multi-professional cooperation with the youth welfare office, psychotherapeutic or school psychology specialists, and possibly also with child and adolescent psychiatry, is of great importance.

In order for these children and young people to participate in inclusive lessons, it is particularly important that teachers do not *act in isolation*. Instead, the team should receive regular supervision or case counselling. The method of *scenic understanding* helps to understand the actions of a child or young person as well as their own behaviour and the feelings that can arise when working with a child (Günther/Bruns 2010, Leber 1983, Gerspach/Katzenbach

1996). This is an important prerequisite for planning educational programmes at school.

In addition, the learning setting at school should enable the child to gradually reduce the symptoms, integrate socially and learn. It is also important to involve classmates and enable them to support the affected pupil as helpers in an age-appropriate manner.

5. Parents who are difficult to reach

5.1 Legal framework for working with parents

In the Federal Republic of Germany the Basic Law [Grundgesetz] stipulates that the care and upbringing of children is the natural right of parents and their duty (Art. 6 Para. 2 GG). The Child and Youth Welfare Act [Kinder und Jugendhilfegesetz] (§1 SGB VIII) also states that every person must have the right and the opportunity to develop into an independent and capable personality (§1 SGB VIII para. 1). If necessary, in Germany the youth welfare services support parents in the realisation of this right, if necessary through educational assistance [*Hilfen zur Erziehung*] (Section 27 SGB VIII).

According to Article 7 Paragraph 1 of the Basic Law, school education is the responsibility of the state. Parental rights limit the rights of the state. Conversely, however, no parental obligations to participate in school education can be derived directly from the Basic Law. Indirectly, it can be concluded from Section 1 of SGB VIII that parents are responsible for their child's success at school if this is jeopardised.

For this reason, the federal states have regulated parental duties and opportunities for parental involvement in their school laws and state constitutions. One example of parental duties is the responsibility to ensure regular school attendance. If this responsibility is not fulfilled, administrative offence proceedings will be initiated after all possibilities for counselling and educational support have been exhausted. In the final instance, fines can be imposed if the obligation to attend school is breached.

A distinction is made between individual and collective parental rights. Individual parental rights include, for example, the right to information about their child's performance. This right is primarily fulfilled through parent-teacher conferences.

Collective parental rights are regulated by the possibility of parental involvement. This can take place at class, school, regional or national level. At federal level, the state parents' councils form the Federal Parents' Council [Bundeselternrat].

The Standing Conference of the Ministers of Education and Cultural Affairs of the Länder in the Federal Republic of Germany [Ständige Konferenz der Kultusminister der Länder in der Bundesrepublik Deutschland – KMK] specifies the understanding of partnership-based cooperation in the *recommendations on education and upbringing as a joint task of parents and schools* (KMK resolution of 11 October 2018) and in the *declaration on the educational partnership between schools and parents* [Erklärung zur Erziehungs-

und Bildungspartnerschaft von Schule und Eltern], which was adopted together with the organisations of people with a migration background (2013). The KMK speaks of education and upbringing as a joint task of schools and parents, of an educational partnership.

5.2 Effect of parents on children's behaviour

The most important tool for changing children's behaviour is not individual support for children but rather joint counselling with parents (Becker 2008, 2019b). Therefore, discussions with parents are the key to success when it comes to understanding children's anxieties and needs and wanting to support children with regard to their emotional and social development. Parents with a diagnosed mental illness or addiction may be exceptions. Another exception is serious cases of child endangerment.

It is important for all children and young people that parents, teachers and other educators work together and provide children with a framework for their emotional and social development (Becker 2019b, Streese/Werning 2021). Depending on the capabilities of the teachers and educational specialists at a school, cooperation can take very different forms.

The heterogeneity between parents reflects the heterogeneity of society. It is important to listen to parents and find out more about their children's living and learning situation. Most parents accept invitations to talks at school. However, there are also parents who do not come to school due to their negative school experience or an individual impairment and prefer to receive teachers at home. In such cases, home visits often lead to a positive turnaround in the co-operation between school and home. As soon as children sense the cooperation of all adult reference persons, the children's behaviour, which is experienced as disruptive at school, can change.

5.3 Hard to reach parents

5.3.1 Causes of difficult accessibility

At the beginning of the school year, in the first few weeks after starting school, parents are often worried and wonder whether their child is doing well at school.

This is reflected in the fact that they accompany their child to the classroom in the morning and pick them up again at the end of the school day, seeking dialogue with the teachers. It is not uncommon for them to call the class teacher in the evening to ask questions about their child's well-being or performance or – from their point of view – to provide important information on how to deal with the child. After the first few weeks of school, these frequent contacts by parents decrease, as they now realise that their child has settled well at school. After that, parents and teachers usually only meet at parents' evenings and consultation days.

Teachers only invite parents to discuss a child in the event of conflicts and difficult educational situations. These may be problems in a child's learning development or incidents or behaviour in which a child is not following the rules or is endangering themselves or others. In this chapter, I would like to deal with the latter.

The reason for the teachers to invite the child to a meeting is usually a negative experience with the child and is therefore exclusively problem-related.

Most teachers want to have conversations with parents that are characterised by mutual respect and cooperation in a spirit of partnership. These teachers want to ask the parents questions and are curious about the parents' answers. They are hoping for tips on how to better deal with the child and want the parents to take their concerns seriously as teachers and look for solutions together with them.

Other teachers hope that the parents will ensure that the challenging behaviour no longer occurs. You try to convey this to the parents concerned in a discussion. You are happy to give the parents tips and expect them to implement them. If parental influence does not lead to a change in the child's behaviour, you would like the parents to seek psychological support or educational assistance from the youth welfare office.

Both ways of organising a discussion with parents can lead to failures in which teachers experience parents as unreachable or difficult to reach (Becker 2019b). This is often the case when

- the socio-economic difference between the teacher and the parents is particularly large,
- parents feel rejected because of their cultural background or religion,
- parents live with a mental illness or addiction,
- one parent is in custody or
- Parents show overprotection towards their children.

5.3.1.1 Socio-economic background

Difficult to reach with high socio-economic status

If teachers invite parents with a high socio-economic status to a problem-related discussion about their child, teachers often describe that parents use their social status to express their superiority over the teachers. In discussions with parents, for example, they may try to prove that teachers have made mistakes in their educational approach or performance assessment, have violated school regulations or have failed in their duty of supervision. Sometimes they also make it clear that they are not dependent on the state school system or inform the teachers that they expect them to solve school problems at school and not to bother them with them. After all, school education is the school's responsibility. Practical school experience shows that parents often threaten to complain about teachers to the school inspectorate and call in a lawyer.

Difficult to reach with low socio-economic status

For the following reasons, a low socio-economic status can make it difficult for educators to reach parents (Harris/Goodall 2008, Medvedev 2020, Stange 2012):

- The parents themselves have had negative experiences at school.
- Parents are unable to attend the school for organisational reasons. Examples include a lack of time (children need to be looked after, shift work, etc.) or a lack of transport.
- Parents' sense of self-efficacy with regard to their ability to support their children at school is low.
- Parents do not feel competent enough to have a conversation with teachers.

Communication in schools in German-speaking countries is largely geared towards parents from the traditional middle class (Reckwitz 2020). With an increase in social disparities in our society, the heterogeneity of parenthood is also increasing (Mevdevev 2020). This leads to the need to break down barriers for parents who do not belong to the traditional middle class (Reckwitz 2020). After the coronavirus pandemic, this is more urgent than ever, as social disparities have increased during this time. The parents of children with impaired emotional and social development are urgently needed as educational partners.

In the perception of teachers, the problem of reaching parents in schools in critical situations has become more acute due to growing social differences. In many federal states, there are now projects in socially deprived areas to promote parental involvement. During the coronavirus pandemic, the sense of community in schools has improved to some extent due to the need for daily consultations.

If parents are to be won over as educational partners in the work with a child who is experienced as difficult, access for these parents must be individualised (Becker 2008, 2019a, 2019b). This means that they must feel welcome by the teachers who invite them, the time and place should be determined taking into account their abilities, the language must be understandable for them without barriers and the aim and content of the conversation must be agreed with them.

5.3.1.2 Subjectively experienced rejection due to cultural origin or religious affiliation

Parents who belong to religious communities or cultures whose way of life and culture are very foreign to teachers in German schools often feel rejected in their children's school community. Schiffauer (2015) analysed this using the example of parents of Muslim faith in Berlin-Kreuzberg. Interviews were conducted with mothers of Muslim faith in a primary school. When they were asked what they thought the rejection they experienced was based on, they gave answers such as: When mothers without headscarves appear in the school playground, they are greeted in a friendly manner by the teachers and the teachers talk to them. The teachers smile at the mothers. When mothers with headscarves come to school, they are also greeted, but neither smiled at nor engaged in conversation. The statements of the mothers of Muslim faith make it clear that the rejection they experience is based less on concrete facts, experiences of discrimination or similar and more on facial expressions, gestures and cordiality.

5.3.1.3 Parents with a mental illness or addiction

Parents with a mental illness or addiction problem are often so preoccupied with solving their own problems that they are unable to give their children enough support in everyday life. Instead, they often find themselves in situations where they are dependent on help. If they live with their child in the same household, the roles in the family are often reversed: The child takes on the role of adult and becomes a helper for parents in difficult situations. In terms of cooperation between parents and teachers, this means that they are unable to fulfil their role of supporting the children in everyday school life. This means that children come to school late or without breakfast, have neither sports kit nor their school materials with them or their homework remains undone. Above all, children want normality in their family. It is therefore important to mobilise parents with mental illness or addiction problems as much as possible as educational partners when their child's behaviour is challenging. As parents with such problems are almost always involved in a system of helpers, it is of central importance for the success of parent-teacher conferences to involve these helpers. If it is not possible to strengthen the parents to fulfil their parenting duties, a decision by the family court may be necessary to place the child in a day group, a residential youth welfare facility or a foster family.

5.3.1.4 Parent in custody

Around 100,000 children in Germany are growing up with at least one parent in custody (Gerbig/Feige 2022). The opportunities to meet up are very limited in terms of time. Visits were temporarily banned during the coronavirus pandemic. Children are worried about their fathers or mothers in custody. They want to be close to them. The children or young people may feel particularly ashamed of their parents being different and not want to talk about it. The result is a family secret that is denied to the school. Frequent explanations are that the absent parent is working abroad or on assignment, is in hospital or at a health resort. It is important to show appreciation and recognition for the achievements of the usually single parent. If there are helpers in the family, they should be included in the discussions in order to relieve the parent who is present and to work out solutions to a school problem together.

5.3.1.5 Parents who show overprotection towards their children

These parents are known in everyday language as *helicopter parents*. They are characterised by overprotection. Behind this overprotection often lie worries and fears. If conversations with parents are to be successful, it is important to recognise and accept these worries and fears. Some mothers define themselves exclusively through their role as a mother. Other mothers and fathers have high performance expectations of their children and worry that their child will not perform well enough at school to maintain their social status. Overprotective parents are happy to attend all school appointments on time or ask for counselling sessions. Teachers are often annoyed by these parents.

The parents described here have little confidence in their child's independence and willingness to take responsibility. For the children, taking responsibility for their own behaviour usually proves to be the key to success. To achieve this, the children need to be empowered. Parents need confidence, security and empowerment to be able to let go and give their children more room for development.

5.3.2 Solutions for conversations with parents

5.3.2.1 General conditions, rules and procedure

General conditions

The framework conditions are crucial for the success of a parent-teacher conference. These include the invitation, the room, the amount of time and the number of participants. If the reason for the parent-teacher conference is challenging behaviour, it is important to focus on concern for the child. This way, parents are not put off or frightened by the invitation alone. All parents are concerned about their child and value it positively when teachers do the same.

Ideally, the date should be agreed with the parents by telephone before the invitation is sent out. An invitation should then be sent by email or post. For data protection reasons, arrangements for meetings with parents should not be sent via social media platforms or WhatsApp. The following aspects should be taken into account when conducting a meeting with parents:

- It is important to choose a room for the counselling session where the conversation can take place undisturbed. Every school should have a counselling room that provides a pleasant atmosphere for the interview.
- The time frame is to be limited to a maximum of 50 minutes.
- If possible, the number of participants from the school should be limited to two people.
- The seating arrangement should be chosen so that everyone sits in a circle or at a 90-degree angle to each other.
- The children and young people should be invited to join in at the end of the discussion so that all adults present can make joint agreements with them and record these in a learning contract.
- A learning contract serves as the basis for the subsequent meeting with parents. This should be agreed at the end of the meeting.

Rules

The discussion is led by the teacher in charge of the class or the head teacher. The aim of the discussion should always be to work together to find solutions to the problem that is causing the teacher concern. It is important to conduct conversations in an appreciative manner. To this end, the teacher leading the discussion should observe the following rules:

- The teacher is curious about the parents' point of view and wants to gain information in order to better understand the meaning of the child's behaviour.
- The participants from the school speak little and listen to the parents. Parents should speak 80 per cent of the time.
- The person conducting the meeting summarises the parents' statements and draws conclusions from them in order to prepare for finding a solution together.
- The conversation rule "I only speak in the first person" applies. School management and teachers should act as role models here. In this way, mutual accusations and justifications can be avoided.
- The meeting ends with a jointly developed solution that is set out in an agreement and the scheduling of a further meeting to evaluate whether the solution has already been successfully implemented or needs to be readjusted.

Procedure

For the course of a parent-teacher conference, it is important that the teachers adopt a professional, positive attitude towards the parents and the child and try to block out negative feelings such as disappointment, anger, rage or helplessness that the child's behaviour has triggered in them. The following phases for parent-teacher conferences have proven to be effective (Bachmair et al. 2014, Faber 2014, 87-91):

- 1st phase: Contact phase

This phase includes the greeting. The greeting *opens the door to* the counselling session and determines the success of the consultation. It is therefore important to pay particular attention to the greeting. If parents are confronted with accusations during the counselling session such as "Your son has (…) again" or "Your daughter is always (…)", they will behave defensively, not disclose any information about the family and end the conversation as quickly as possible. Or they will try to defend their child and reproach the teachers. This applies all the more to parents who come to a parent-teacher conference at school anxious.

A warm welcome is therefore very important to ensure a positive start to the conversation. After a sentence such as "I'm glad you're here!" and a brief small talk, the transition to the problem phase should take place.

If parents are late, there are usually important reasons for this and the parents had to make a special effort to come to the school for the interview. It is important to ask about the reasons and let the parents talk about their problems in order to show appreciation for the parents.

- 2nd phase: Problem phase

In the second phase, it makes sense to first present the strengths and positive characteristics of the child that the teacher perceives, before naming the reason for the conversation: "I'm worried about your child because (…)". By introducing the topic in this way, parents sense the teacher's interest in their child's well-being. They can build trust and add their perspective on the problem. If the parents do not present their perspective on their own initiative, the teacher should ask them to do so. It is important to listen to the parents and gather information during this part of the conversation. At the end, the teacher summarises what information they have gained from the parents.

- 3rd phase: Structural phase

In the structure phase, the teacher relates the information obtained from the parents to the child's challenging behaviour so that a common understanding of the child's needs can be established. ☐ 4th phase: Contract phase

All parties involved work together to find a solution. An agreement is reached with a maximum of three agreements, which may be recorded in writing and signed by everyone, including the child. The agreements must be as specific and small-step as possible. The more concrete the solutions are, the greater the success. If possible, the child or young person should be actively involved in the contract phase or informed of the outcome at the end.

5.3.2.2 Case studies

Parents with high socio-economic status: Jens

Jens (8) attends the early years phase in his first year at school. He learns to read and write very quickly. He can concentrate well on learning content and performs well in maths. However, his behaviour is in contrast to his academic performance. When the class teacher comes into the classroom in the morning, Jens jumps up in front of her without touching her, making noises like a lion and shouting: "I'll kill you!" "I'll eat you!". He also frightens other children by attacking them and shouting that he will kill them. The teacher invites the parents in for a chat. They report that he does not show any abnormal behaviour at home, not even when playing with his older sister. The parents listen to the teacher's concerns. They describe that they work at home as book authors and are therefore always available for their children. The parents suggest consulting the school psychologist and thank the teacher for the conversation.

After classroom observation and family discussions between the school psychology specialist and the parents, the mother and father understand that although they are present at home all day, they are not interested enough in Jens' school performance and the activities at school and therefore only speak to him regularly out of a sense of duty. They do not go to the Christmas party or the school summer party. Their interest in school is only awakened by the teacher's description of their son's aggressive behaviour. The boy learns that his negative behaviour at school attracts the attention of his parents, who would otherwise only pay attention to their books. An agreement is reached that the parents will not work from 5.00-8.00 p.m. every day, but will play, read, listen to reports from school and eat together with the children during this time. As a result, Jens' challenging behaviour decreases.

Parents with low socio-economic status: Siri

Siri (14) is the oldest of six children and is in eighth grade. Her school attendance is irregular. It is particularly noticeable that she attends less and less in the second half of the month and then always seems tired, quickly feels provoked by others and gets into conflicts. The teacher makes several telephone appointments with the mother for a meeting and sends an invitation by post. The parents do not attend the appointment. When the teacher calls the parents, they apologise and say they have forgotten the appointment.

The teacher makes another appointment and calls the parents one hour before the meeting and says: "I am pleased that we are meeting today at 2.00 pm." The parents then turn up on time. During the conversation, it turns out that both parents have problems reading the invitation letter as they are illiterate and are also unable to orientate themselves in terms of time. The teacher tells the parents that she is worried about Siri's frequent absences and tiredness at school. As she listens to the parents, she learns that the citizen's benefit only last until the middle of the month, which is why they can hardly buy any food after that. The children are then hungry, tired and feel ill, which is why they miss school. The class teacher suggests that the parents apply for family support, which they gladly accept. Family support is provided by the youth welfare office and helps the parents to organise their everyday lives. Siri now attends school regularly.

Presumption of religious differences: Emir

Emir (13) is a pupil in year eight at a grammar school. The class has new teachers in all subjects and a new class teacher for this school year. In physics, Emir catches the eye of the subject teacher, Mr Meider. Emir leaves the classroom several times a lesson to go and wash his hands during the lesson. Every time Mr Meider wants to start with an input on a topic, Emir blows his nose loudly and gets up to take his handkerchief to the bin.

Mr Meider asks him several times to blow his nose quietly, to which Emir replies that he is allowed to blow his nose, even in class. Mr Meider sees Emir as cheeky and provocative. He tells Emir that he will call his parents to talk to them about Emir's behaviour. Emir replies with a laugh: "You can call my father. He won't answer because he doesn't have time. He's always at the mosque. And if he does answer the phone, he'll tell you that only the mosque is important and not school. School doesn't matter. He might even report them if I tell him that they won't let me blow my nose."

Mr Meider does not call the parents at first and continues to try to ignore Emir's behaviour. When his disruption of lessons increases, he asks the class teacher to invite the parents to a meeting.

The class teacher reaches Emir's father on the first call and invites both parents to a meeting at the school. His mother is currently staying with her parents in Turkey and is unable to attend. The class teacher, the physics teacher and the father are present at the meeting. Emir is asked to join them after thirty minutes. The class teacher greets the father and informs him that the teachers are worried about Emir because he is displaying behaviour that is damaging the family's reputation. The father is shocked and thanks them for the invitation. The class teacher emphasises that she wants to find a solution together with him as the father. The father agrees. The teachers describe the situation from the physics lesson. The father laughs and says that he is not a devout Muslim, would never go to the mosque or observe Ramadan. His children's education is very important to him and he wants his son to graduate from high school.

The teachers and the father are pursuing the same goal. They agree that the father will tell Emir in the presence of the teachers that he must behave in class in such a way that neither his classmates nor the teachers are disturbed by him. After the father makes this announcement, Emir apologises to Mr Meider. The disruptions in physics lessons no longer occur.

Parents with addiction: Thorsten and Elena

Thorsten (14) is often absent from school. When he comes to school, he behaves quietly and inchallengingly. The teacher cannot reach the single mother by phone or post and decides, together with the school social work specialist, to make a home visit after school. Thorsten's younger brother opens the front door. As there is no adult to be seen, they go into the flat and call out. Thorsten is in the kitchen and is putting oatmeal with milk on the table for his younger siblings. The school social work specialist and the teacher ask about his mother. Thorsten says she's asleep but sets off to fetch her. After ten minutes, Thorsten's mum comes staggering into the kitchen. She shouts: "What's going on here?" The teacher tells her that she is worried because neither Thorsten comes to school nor is she available as a mum. The mum says: "I'm not surprised that Thorsten doesn't go to school. He's a good-for-nothing like his father. You can see how much I have to do with the four children. I'm all on my own. I always tell Thorsten to go to school, but what am I supposed to do if he doesn't go?"

The mother reports that the youth welfare office wants to take the children away from her if she doesn't stop drinking. The caseworker says: "It's important that Thorsten goes to school so that the children can stay with them." The class teacher adds: "We can take Thorsten to school with us straight away. If he comes to class regularly for five days, we'll confirm his school attendance in writing for the youth welfare office." "Yes, that's good. Take him straight away." The teacher then says to Thorsten's mum: "I would like to invite you and the social worker from the youth welfare office to a meeting so that we can talk about Thorsten's support. Would you be willing to come to the school for such a meeting?" "Yes, if I can bring the other boys with me."

Elena (6) has been attending a first grade class for nine months. Elena is frequently absent. Her mother has provided excuses for all absences. The teachers are in close dialogue with the single mother, who tells them eloquently and in lengthy conversations about Elena's symptoms and the doctors' concerns that she may "have a serious illness. The symptoms described by the mother range from abdominal pain and headaches to a very high fever with severe vomiting. The teachers fully understand Elena's mother, but still find the number of sick days very noticeable. Overall, Elena only attended lessons for twelve days in the first eight months of school.

In a discussion with the school social worker, the idea is developed to introduce Elena to the child and youth health service, especially as it has now been established that she has never attended the school medical check-up. The mother takes a critical view of this, but agrees to it. No symptoms can be found there that would indicate a serious health impairment. In a conversation with the doctor, the mother talks about her alcohol addiction and how she can't get up in the morning to wake Elena up and get her ready for school. This is why she calls in her daughter sick almost every day. With the mother's agreement, contact is made with the youth welfare office. The mother receives educational support and a therapy place in the day clinic.

Parents in custody: Andreas

Andreas (12) lives from year 1 to 6 in an inpatient facility with an associated residential school. Andreas does not exhibit any challenging behaviour there. Accompanied by the youth welfare office, he has regular contact with his parents, who are now separated. In seventh grade, he returns to his mother after she marries for the second time. The mother's new living conditions appear so stable to the youth welfare office that she is allowed to take Andreas back in. The biological father has been sentenced to seven years in prison for assault.

Andreas feels comfortable at his new comprehensive school near his home. However, he insults male classmates on the way to school and in his free time on the street without any previous conflict and starts fights. The class teacher asks the mother and Andreas for a meeting. The mother brings the family support worker with her. During the meeting, the class teacher expresses her concern for Andreas. Parents of other boys in the class consider pressing criminal charges against him.

During the conversation, it emerges that Andreas misses his father. The visits to the prison are only planned at long intervals and have been cancelled several times due to the coronavirus. It becomes clear that Andreas feels close to his father when he is aggressive and beats him up. Then he feels strong. As a result of the conversation, it is agreed that his father should be visited more frequently and regularly in prison.

When Andreas learns that he can now meet his father more often and a date has already been set for his visit, the insults towards other young people and the instigating of fights stop.

5.4 Conclusion

If parents are difficult for teachers or educational professionals to reach, there are always important reasons for this, which usually lie in the parents' life situation. The aim of parent-teacher conferences at school is to improve support for the child. In this respect, it is important to create a trusting framework for parent-teacher conferences and to gain an understanding of the parents' situation in order to be able to work out solutions together to improve the child's situation at school. This chapter presents rules and a tried-and-tested procedure for achieving these goals.

6. Prevention of challenging behaviour and conflicts

6.1 Prevention of challenging behaviour

The case studies presented in chapters 2 to 5 show that teachers can become projection surfaces for pupils and their parents in everyday school life. Conversely, teachers and socio-educational professionals unconsciously bring their biographical experiences into their educational work (Gerspach/Katzenbach 1996). When children process traumatic experiences, the associated fears can be expressed through unconscious *negative transference* in the form of disruptions to lessons or other forms of challenging behaviour.

Challenging behaviour, disruptions in lessons and conflicts can be counteracted preventively through educational structures in the school, a school policy, school rules, clear classroom management and rules and rituals in everyday classroom life. If the school policy is developed in a participatory manner with all members of the school community and is based on mutual respect, discrimination and thus occasions for offence as triggers for challenging behaviour are reduced. If a school policy contains clear rules that are supported by all members of the school community, these rules represent a boundary that is usually adhered to even when children and young people are aggressively defending themselves against anxieties or can at least be used to reflect on behaviour following conflict situations. For this reason, the school policy and the school rules form a framework that can be used to successfully counteract challenging behaviour in a preventative educational manner.

6.2 School policy

In order for a school policy to have a positive effect, it is of central importance that the entire school community is involved in its development and that the school policy is actively lived. This means that in addition to the teachers and school management, parents, pupils, the administrative staff in the secretariat, the cook, the school assistants, the school caretaker and other educational professionals must be involved in the development of the school policy. The development process should be moderated by a steering group and, if necessary, by an external consultant.

It is important that the process is based on a time-measurement plan and that the current planning status is always visible to all participants.

The development of a school policy begins with an analysis of the school's current situation. This is followed by the development of a vision, which should motivate identification with the school and work on the school concept. The conclusion should be duly celebrated, published on the homepage and communicated to the public of the neighbourhood in which the school is located through the media (Becker/Brunswicker 2020).

The core of the school policy is the mission statement. It should be developed after the common vision has been formulated. The mission statement should express that all pupils are welcome regardless of their origin, competences and language. The winners of the German School Award meet this requirement with their school policies. Two winners of the German School Award 2022 have committed to the following mission statements:

"We see ourselves as a school in which every child, regardless of their background and ability, can live and learn together and receive the individual support they need. Our aim is to prepare competent and self-confident children for the challenges of the future" (Havelmüller Primary School 2022) [translated by the author].

"The comprehensive school for all pupils: regardless of their abilities, talents and recommendations. We accept children of all abilities, from a wide range of social and cultural backgrounds, with and without special needs. We support and advise all pupils individually. We experience diversity as enrichment!" (Comprehensive School Münster-Mitte 2021) [translated by the author].

In the school policy, the mission statement and the analysis of the current situation are followed in the table of contents by development projects on teaching, opening the school to the outside world, cooperation with parents as educational partners, all-day schooling, working together, the experience of democracy, school life, dealing with and using media and sustainability. The development projects are backed up with goals, measures for implementation and evaluation plans.

At all-day schools, these children and young people benefit in particular from tiered houses, in which classrooms and all-day rooms for up to three year groups are close together in one building or part of a building. As poverty increases, so does the number of children with malnutrition. Particularly in the second half of the month, recipients of unemployment benefit II, social benefit or citizen's allowance increasingly go without fresh fruit and vegetables. Malnutrition affects the learning development and behaviour of children and young people. For children growing up in poor families, a free school breakfast and lunch are important prerequisites for learning at school.

To prevent challenging behaviour and conflicts, it is particularly important to reliably anchor rules and structures for social interaction in everyday school life. Procedures for conflict resolution should be mentioned here, such as: The Stop Rule, mediation, the dispute mediators and the schoolyard buddies. In addition, the "dispute carpet" method was developed for the primary level: "If both parties agree, the carpet is rolled out, the affected parties take a seat on it and the rest of the class, including adults, spread out on the outside. The children talk about their dispute using 'I' messages and facing each other. Only then are the spectators involved and asked whether they have understood the conflict and whether there are any questions or observers of the dispute. If the disputants have not found a solution to resolve their conflict themselves, the other children are asked for ideas" (Havelmüller Primary School 2022).

To promote social interaction, conflict resolution and the experience of democracy, class councils, pupil parliaments and pupil assemblies should be mentioned (Friedrichs 2023). It is important that children and young people are supported in their implementation and that educational specialists are available for this purpose. In many federal states, youth education programmes offer workshops for children and young people who are involved in student representation. It is also important that student councils are given a budget and the opportunity to use media.

If structures for promoting cooperation and experiencing democracy are anchored in the school policy and lived out in everyday school life, children and young people learn to articulate their fears, worries and needs. They experience appreciation and empathy from their fellow pupils. This enables them to find solutions together. This increases their sense of self-efficacy. Children and young people feel strong, develop fewer fears and are less likely to exhibit challenging behaviour. In this respect, a school policy based on mutual respect has a preventative effect on conflicts and promotes living and learning in democratic structures.

6.3 School rules

The school policy should provide support and orientation with clear rules and set boundaries to prevent danger and impairment of well-being. It is important that the rules are clearly formulated and justified. Young people in particular must not be given the impression that adults are arbitrarily imposing rules. If pupils are not involved, young people in particular will be provoked to rebel against them. The school rules should therefore be developed with all those involved in the school community in order to ensure identification with the school rules.

> Certain school rules of the Refik Veseli School Berlin
> (integrated secondary school with upper secondary school)
>
> "Every child should be recognised in their individual personality and encouraged, supported and nurtured on the basis of their individual goals, learning requirements and biographical experiences. It is also important to recognise the weaknesses of each child. Diversity is a source of learning at our school. We want every child to be able to realise the best possible school-leaving qualification for them.
>
> The focus of education is on helpfulness and respect for fellow students, teachers and other members of the school community. Exemplary performance and social behaviour are praised, and active action is taken against all forms of violence, discrimination and exclusion (e.g. bullying) (Art. 2 of the Basic Law). Teachers and parents work closely together in the education of young people.
>
> Any form of verbal or physical violence towards others is prohibited. The disregard of school rules is first addressed in a discussion with a teacher and in the class council. An effort to make amends should be developed and implemented. The reparation should be directly related to the disregarded school rule (e.g. painting a wall in case of deliberate soiling). The reparation must be documented and should be evaluated in the class council. If the educational measures have no effect, disciplinary measures will be taken" (Refik Veseli School 2017) [translated by the author].

At the Refik Veseli School, the Pestalozzi-Fröbel-Haus, the independent youth welfare organisation for school social work, has introduced a peer to peer consultation. Pupils can come to the school representatives to talk about their problems. In addition to this, the student representatives have a weekly meeting with the school management about breaches of the school rules or other conflicts affecting fellow pupils for which they have been unable to find a solution themselves.

A working group of Reckahn has spent three years developing the Reckahn Rulebook for Young and Old Children – Living and Learning with Children's Rights. It is based on the Reckahn Reflections – On the Ethics of Educational Relationships (Prengel 2017, Prengel 2022). The Reckahn Reflections are guidelines for educational action that aim to strengthen mutual respect for the dignity of all members of schools and institutions. The guidelines encourage reflection and serve as orientation for long-term professional development at the relationship level in educational institutions. The rule booklet serves to promote human rights education and democratic education. It contains twelve rules that can be added to by any school class or school community that works with it (Prengel/Maywald 2020, Prengel 2022). The rule booklet is available to download from Rochow Academy and can also be obtained there (Prengel/Maywald 2020). It is suitable for working with school classes on rule violations.

When rules are broken, the focus must be on reflecting on the behaviour shown and making amends. Making amends enables all children and young people to learn from a conflict, experience appreciation and remain part of the school or class community. Here is an example of reparation (for further examples, see chapters 2.3.3 and 3.2.6):

Svea and Swantje

Svea (10) is sitting next to Swantje. Swantje (9) has beautiful handwriting and has just written a two-page essay in her German lesson. Svea has already made several attempts and is unhappy with the results. She takes Swantje's essay, crumples it up and tears it up. In a subsequent conflict resolution meeting between the class representatives, Swantje and Svea, Svea apologises and the following reparation is agreed: Svea collects the scraps of paper again and sticks the text back together. She then scans it and provides Swantje with a printout of her text. Svea explains to the teacher why the text has been crumpled up and damaged and asks for Swantje's essay to be accepted.

6.4 Conclusion

The school policy and school rules ensure the well-being of all members of the school community, create a framework for respectful interaction with one another and prevent challenging behaviour through structures in everyday school life. In this way, conflicts are reduced. Feedback discussions between teachers, parents and pupils (Chapter 1) supplement structures for social interaction. Nevertheless, there are children and young people who require additional structures for support and social stabilisation due to significant impairments in their emotional and social development. The following chapter is dedicated to these pupils with special educational needs.

7. Learning accesses for pupils with special needs in their emotional and social development

7.1 Inclusive and exclusive currents

In the Federal Republic of Germany, the percentage of pupils with identified special educational needs in the area of emotional and social development who receive inclusive education has risen sharply, from 15.7 per cent in 2008 to 54.7 per cent in 2020 (KMK 2012 and 2022). However, if we look at the absolute number of pupils with special educational needs in the area of emotional and social development, we see that this has increased in Germany from 55,442 in 2008 to 103,571 in 2022 (KMK 2012, KMK 2022, Becker, 2013; Stein, 2011).

With the increase in absolute numbers of children with special educational needs in their emotional and social development, the number of pupils in joint lessons has risen from 9,200 in 2009 to 59,477 in 2020 (Becker, 2021b, KMK 2022, Stein, 2011).

At the same time, the number of pupils at special schools for educational needs in Germany also increased. In Germany, it rose from 25,702 in 2000 to 44,094 in 2020. Looking back, the figures collected for Germany (as a whole) (KMK 2022) can be summarised as follows: a percentage reduction in the number of children and young people in special schools has been made possible by the increase in the total number of pupils with this specialisation.

If we look at the developments in individual federal states, we see that they vary greatly from region to region. Berlin, Brandenburg, Bremen, Hamburg and Thuringia deviate from the overall trend described for Germany. In these federal states, it has been possible to reduce the number of pupils with special needs in their emotional and social development who are taught in special schools. In Schleswig-Holstein, the number of pupils taught in special schools remained the same between 2008/2009 and 2016/2017 (Döttinger 2018). In summary, it can be stated that despite the ratification of the General Assembly *Convention on the Rights of Persons with Disabilities* in Germany on 24 February 2009, strong tendencies towards separation can be observed in the special needs area of emotional and social development alongside inclusive tendencies (Döttinger 2018). The following section presents a support approach that succeeds in transforming segregating tendencies into inclusive tendencies in school practice for children with significant impairments in emotional and social development.

7.2 Transition project

7.2.1 Theoretical background

The term *transition* goes back to the work of the British child and adolescent psychiatrist D. W. Winnicott. He developed the theory of *transitional objects* (Becker 1995a, 2008). Adults develop musical or artistic activities in an *intermediate world*, in a so-called intermediate space. Transitional *objects* are precursors to musical or artistic activities. Young children develop a *transitional object* in the intermediate space in order to bridge temporary separations from their primary caregiver. "In order for it to function as a comforter, the child must be able to *charge* an object such as the teddy bear with illusions. The ability to form illusions depends on whether the child has gained trust in the relationship with the mother. This is only possible if the child receives so much maternal care in the early relationship that the illusion of omnipotence can develop in the child" (Becker 1995a, 67, Winnicott 2023) [translated by the author].

For example, a teddy bear or rag doll can comfort a two-year-old child and give them courage when their primary carer has dropped them off at the daycare centre in the morning and is not available during the day. The *transitional object* helps the child to reduce separation anxieties and enables them to feel at ease in the daycare centre and learn through play. The *Transition project* utilises the principle of the *transitional object*. It is a school-based support approach that focuses on educational relationships rather than content. The object of learning in the classroom becomes a *transitional object* for the child within the educational relationship and enables the child to concentrate on learning at school. Developing the effect of such triangulation is challenging and complex. In order for this to succeed, all those involved need to learn. This applies to teachers, educational professionals, the child concerned, parents and classmates. This opens up a new approach between the adults and the affected child, which often leads to the challenging behaviour becoming superfluous. The structures that are needed in everyday school life in order to teach these children in an inclusive school are called *learning accesses*.

7.2.2 Study results

Experience in individual federal states such as Hamburg and Bremen, as well as in inclusive schools in other federal states, shows that it is possible to reverse the trend towards segregated education for children with special needs in their emotional and social development. This is possible if teachers, children and parents receive enough support to accept and appreciate the inclusive educational programme. The *Transition project* provides the conditions for this. Studies from several years (Becker 2006, 2012a, 2014 and 2016b) show that this support approach also allows children who are considered *unable to* remain in their local school and be taught in joint lessons. The support approach is suitable for pupils in years 1 to 8.

In the third study on the *Transition project,* which was carried out in 2016, 58 class leaders from primary and secondary schools in Berlin were surveyed using semi-standardised questionnaires on changes in the behaviour of the children that was dangerous to others and to themselves taught in the *Transition project* (2019a).

These were exclusively pupils who, without this programme, would very likely have had to switch to a school replacement project run by youth welfare services. At the time the teachers were surveyed, 32 children in Berlin had been supported for six to twelve months and 26 children for 18 to 24 months in the *Transition project* (Becker 2019a, 13) [translated by the author]. The evaluation shows that all children who were supported in the *Transition project* were able to remain at their home school. The results of the study also show that, according to the teachers' assessment, almost all pupils were able to significantly reduce their dangerous behaviour towards others and themselves during the support period: "At the beginning of the support in August 2015, the teachers frequently observed dangerous behaviour towards others or themselves in 20 pupils. Three children rarely exhibit this behaviour and nine pupils do not. After twelve months of support, only four pupils were still frequently observed by the class teachers to exhibit behaviour that was dangerous to others or themselves, 16 children rarely exhibited such behaviour and twelve pupils no longer exhibited such behaviour" (Becker 2019a, 13) [translated by the author]. The survey of the pupils who received support for 18 to 24 months in the *Transition project* revealed the following results: At the beginning of the support, 20 out of 32 pupils frequently exhibited behaviour that was dangerous to others or themselves. "After 18 to 24 months of support, the teachers only frequently observed other- or self-endangering behaviour in four pupils, rarely in 16 children and no longer at all in twelve pupils" (Becker 2019a, 13) [translated by the author].

7.2.3 Internal school organisation

In the *Transition project,* a support group consisting of four to six children is formed as a temporary learning group to supplement the classroom lessons. The project is suitable for pupils in years one to eight. A special needs teacher or a teacher who is interested in the task assumes responsibility for the implementation of the five *learning accesses* for the entire support group. In addition, they organise the diagnostics to determine special educational needs and support planning, which is anchored in the *Transition project* through regular consultations. Written support planning must be carried out regularly for all pupils with special educational needs. The form and frequency is regulated in the regulations on special educational needs of the federal states. The teacher in charge of the temporary learning group, known as the *transition class,* is allocated time for the *Transition project.* This should be agreed within the school.

The children in the support group continue to attend lessons in their regular class. Class leaders can nominate a child for the temporary learning group. The prerequisite for admission is an identified special educational need or an impairment that is comparable to this. In addition, the pupils have a need for educational support (SGB VIII).

These children or adolescents may be pupils with a *basic disorder* or a *basic fault* (Becker 2022b, Lempp 2006): "The children and adolescents affected by this show a pronounced inability to socialise and a simultaneous hunger for contact, which leads to them constantly seeking relationships, but soon letting them fail again due to excessive demands and one-sided stress. They are only able to adapt to the wishes and concerns of those around them to a limited extent, are barely able to do without in favour of someone else, constantly seek recognition and love and then destroy these through their dissocial and provocative behaviour. Their rebellious and aggressive behaviour causes considerable educational difficulties even in childhood. They push themselves to the fore and seek attention at all costs and would obviously rather be punished than ignored. This behaviour corresponds to a weakness of attachment, even a lack of attachment, which then very often turns into dissocial and criminal behaviour as they get older" (Lempp 2006, 46) [translated by the author].

For these children and young people with particularly challenging behaviour, selective multi-professional meetings between all educational professionals and teachers is not enough. Rather, you need a multi-professional team of at least three professional reference persons who are available to the children and young people within a fixed time frame with supportive educational relationships. This is made possible in the *Transition project.*

Parents must be in agreement with admission to the group. The decision is made by the whole school, school level or year group conference. The length of stay is six to 24 months. Confidentiality is agreed for all individual discussions that go beyond the usual information about pupils.

7.2.4 *Exchange and dissemination*

Exchange

In Berlin, Hamburg, Bremen, Brandenburg, Nordrhein-Westfalen, Thüringen, Niedersachsen, Sachsen, Switzerland and Luxembourg, training courses and specialist days on the *Transition project* were organised. In Hamburg, Bremen and Brandenburg, temporary learning groups are being implemented to support pupils with significant behavioural impairments. In this context, schools work according to the educational concept of the *Transition project* or comparable concepts. These include family classes (Wuntke et al. 2023) or *Developmental Teaching* (ETEP) (Bergson/Luckfield 1998, Wood 1996). In other federal states that have carried out further training on *Transition project,* the concept is being implemented in individual schools.

Supra-regional specialist events between participants from the city states have been taking place since 2015. The meeting was suspended due to the coronavirus and took place again for the first time on 23.03.23 with participants from Hamburg, Berlin, Sachsen, Thüringen and Brandenburg in Bremen as a symposium on temporary learning groups at the Bürgerzentrum Neue Vahr (LIS Bremen 2023).

In the following, the distribution of learning groups working on the basis of the *Transition project* or comparable concepts in Berlin, Hamburg and Bremen will be presented:

Berlin

In 1998, the *Transition Project* was launched as a joint project of the

Senate Department for Education, Youth and Sport, the Institute for Intercultural Education at the Free University of Berlin, the school psychology service in Berlin-Tempelhof-Schöneberg and the PrignitzSchule support centre and initially implemented at the Werbellinsee primary school in Berlin. From 2000 to 2020, the support approach will be multiplied via the Berlin regional training programme and supported with case consultations.

In the 2011/2012 school year, this approach was successfully practised in some schools in seven Berlin districts and was incorporated into Berlin's overall concept for inclusive schools. The following development can be observed since 2012: The *Transition project* setting has found its way into the educational practice of many schools without being explicitly mentioned as such. Various names such as transition, tiger, pirate or bridge classes are used in the schools involved in the further training and evaluation of *Transition project.* The teachers in these groups are in close dialogue with teachers from other concepts, e.g. developmental therapy or developmental education (Bergson/Luckfield 1998) or family classes (Wuntke/Blumenthal/Köhler/Mahlau 2023) and give each other suggestions. In the school year 2019/2020 43 schools in Berlin worked on the educational basis of the *Transition project.* Since 1999, the teachers involved have been supported by training and counselling services provided by the Verband Sonderpädagogik Berlin e.V., cooperating independent youth welfare organisations and Fortbildung Berlin. Network meetings are also organised.

Hamburg

In Hamburg, a framework agreement on regional cooperation between schools and youth welfare services for the education and care of children and young people with particularly challenging behaviour was concluded in 2013 between the Ministry of Schools and Vocational Training and the Ministry of Labour, Health, Social Affairs, Family and Integration (Social Welfare Department). This agreement sets out the framework for the establishment of integrative (school-integrated) and temporary learning groups. To organise the cooperation agreement, 300 places in the school-integrated learning groups and 100 places for the external temporary learning groups are provided each year. The programmes accept children and young people throughout the year (Ehlers 2014).

In 2021, 392 pupils attended a school-integrated temporary learning group. The support programme was completed for 289 children or young people. Of these, 149 pupils were fully reintegrated into a regular class at a mainstream school. For 127 pupils, reintegration into the mainstream school took place. In the meantime, 22 children and young people have changed schools. The change of school was partly due to educational reasons and partly due to relocation (Ehlers 2023).

In Hamburg, the coronavirus pandemic has shown that the temporary learning group programme has ensured support for children and young people and their parents during the crisis. During the second lockdown, there was hardly any outreach youth support from the youth welfare offices. Within the temporary learning groups, the children and young people who had a place there were provided with flexible services in such a way that almost 100 per cent contact could be ensured. During the pandemic, counselling was provided in direct contact, by telephone or online to avoid overburdening parents and guardians. Parents approached the specialists in the temporary learning groups with a wide range of concerns, such as the provision of food for their children, psychological emergencies, child protection issues, the implementation of necessary hygiene measures and the use of mobile devices (Ehlers 2023).

Bremen

In Bremen, temporary learning groups were set up at 23 schools in the 2022/2023 school year. They work on the basis of the five *learning accesses* in the *Transition project* or according to comparable concepts. The schools cooperate closely with the Regional Care and Support Centres (ReBUZ) and the Office for Social Services. The State Institute for Schools makes a decisive contribution to the success of the support for the children and parents concerned. The support takes the form of specialist events, network meetings and ongoing support for the people responsible for implementing the programme.

The support takes place regionally in cooperation with the regional advice and support centres.

7.3 Five learning accesses

In the *Transition project,* five *learning accesses* are implemented as fixed structures in the daily routine of a school, creating space and time for relationship work. This creates a setting for educational work in which positive aspects of the relationship between the teacher and the child come into effect in such a way that challenging behaviour can be reduced for the children concerned and learning at school can become possible again. The following organisational structures have proven successful in inclusive schools (Becker/Prengel 2016b).

Five learning accesses to successful inclusive education
- Inclusive teaching
- Temporary learning group *transition class*
- Counselling in a multi-professional team
- Counselling with parents
- Cooperation between schools and youth welfare services (Becker/Prengel 2016b)

7.3.1 Temporary learning group

The temporary learning group takes place four times a week for 90 minutes. The four to six pupils leave their school class to be supported in the third and fourth periods in a mixed-age temporary learning group organised across classes. The children can invite other pupils from their school class to join the temporary learning group on a fixed day of the week.

The temporary learning group serves to relieve the burden on teachers and classmates and to provide individual support for children with special needs (Becker 2019, 10-14).

Interior design

A room is required for the temporary learning group, which is set up according to a special room concept (Becker 2019, 10-14): "Each child has a *pupil's office,* which is spatially demarcated with crepe strips on the floor, shelves and possibly a cupboard. The pupil sets up the *pupil's office* themselves with the support of the teacher. There are binding office rules for everyone in the *class.*

According to these rules, classmates and teachers may only enter the individual *pupil's offices* when requested to do so by the owner of the *pupil's office*" (Becker 2019, 11). There is a shared group table for all children in the group as well as studios (work corners) for working, researching and experimenting. Ideally, the work studio consists of a workbench with tools and wood scraps.

Lessons are led by the teacher responsible for the *Transition project*. The lessons follow a fixed schedule.

Exemplary procedure: Temporary learning group (Becker 2019, 11)

1. Phase: Basic support (20 min/group table)
2. Phase: Concentration and perception (20 min./group table)
3. Phase: Learning on own topic or free day learning (20 min./in the student office)
4. Phase: Work on tasks on basic maths and language skills from the class (20 min./student office)
5. Phase: Games for social learning (10 min.)

It is important that lessons in the temporary learning group do not begin with traditional teaching materials or media, such as a textbook, workbook or blackboard. Instead, materials for basic support that are highly stimulating should be provided for the children. For example, wooden cubes in various sizes, an arithmetic train, a car quartet, the *golden bead material* or *number stars for the multiplication tables are* suitable for basic support in maths.

In the second phase, activities are offered to promote perception and concentration. Individual tasks from the *Marburg concentration training* (Krowatschek 2019) or concentration games such as Mikado can be used for these phases. From year 5 onwards, technical drawing with a drawing board has proven to be a good way to promote perception and concentration in a career-orientated way.

In the third phase of the temporary learning group, the pupils work on their own topics. In this phase, each child chooses a non-school topic in which they are interested. Ideally, this should be a topic related to crafts or research. For example, children like to build an object out of wood. This could be an aeroplane or a ship. The results of their work on their own topics are documented and regularly presented to the class.

In the fourth phase, each child works independently with the support of the teacher in their *pupil's office* on tasks set by the class teacher. If possible, they work with weekly plans or on learning office tasks.

It is important that the teacher in the *transition class* only takes on auxiliary ego functions (cf. 4.2.6) and that the class teacher assigns and evaluates the tasks to the child so that they remain the person in authority. This means that the teacher of the *transition class* does not demand the completion of the tasks, but supports the child in completing the work assignments for the class teacher.

To do this, they can ask questions such as: "Mrs Müller expects you to hand in the tasks from the weekly plan tomorrow. So far you have only completed one of five tasks. How can I support you?" The following case study illustrates the education in the *Transition project*.

Yegor

Yegor (8) spends a lot of class time under the table. He refuses to come out and work on written assignments. This is why the *Transition project* comes into question for him. After six months in the *Project class, the* following situation arises: Yegor is very interested in woodworking at the workbench. He builds an aeroplane with the help of the *teacher*. When the teacher then asks him about his tasks from the weekly timetable for his school class, he shouts: "The stupid weekly timetable!". He hits the workbench several times with a broomstick. The teacher asks him how he intends to deal with the fact that he doesn't feel like doing maths, but that the teacher wants to see his weekly timetable, which should be as complete as possible, today.

Yegor calms down, thinks, but doesn't answer the teacher. She suggests that he cut out five problems from each of the worksheets and only calculate these. Yegor beams and immediately starts working on the five problems quickly and independently in his pupil's office. He brings the worksheet to the teacher, who praises him. He then immediately starts calculating the five problems on the second worksheet, beaming with joy.

At the end of the next school day, he brings the aeroplane he has built to the class teacher and explains to the class how he built it. Other children immediately come forward who want to join the *transition class as guests* to build an aeroplane too. Yegor is allowed to choose the child who will join him in the group as a guest child.

The class teacher is delighted that Yegor has calculated five problems from each worksheet. The teacher of the *transition class* and the class teacher discuss with Gregor that he should calculate ten tasks per worksheet in the next week, which he succeeds in doing.

7.3.2 Inclusive teaching

Pupils who are supported in the *Transition project* take part in lessons in their school class as much as possible. In this way, they can utilise positive role models from their classmates (Becker 2019; Bless/Müller 2017). "The younger the children are, the greater the impact of positive peer influences" (Becker 2019, 10) [translated by the author]. When preparing lessons, it is particularly important to provide the child from the *transition class with* individualised support to enable them to learn in class. In addition, individualised support for other children with support needs should also be taken into account in the planning and implementation of lessons. In this way, not only the children in the *transition class* but also other children benefit from the inclusion educational expertise of the teacher leading the *transition class*, and there are further training effects for the class teacher and the subject teachers.

7.3.3 Counselling in a multi-professional team

Pupils who are included in the *Transition project* sometimes require support throughout their school day. For the inclusive education of these children to succeed, it is important that everyone who works with a child at school develops a shared understanding of the case and harmonises their educational activities accordingly. In this context, we speak of a multi-professional team. This team requires regular case counselling or supervision in order to be able to reflect on their educational actions with regard to the child's development (Becker 2022; Gerspach/Katzenbach 1996, Streese/Werning 2021, Würker 2007, Zimmermann/Würker 2023).

"Collegial case counselling or supervision open up the possibility of reflecting on children's development in such a way that the professional reference persons can provide support, set boundaries and take on ego functions for pupils: Pupils with impairments in emotional development relieve themselves by transferring aspects of parental reference persons to the various professionals in the school. If the teachers identify with these attributions, this can (…) lead to splitting in the team" (Becker 2022b, 66) [translated by the author].

Through case counselling or supervision, teachers and educational specialists receive support that enables them to successfully teach pupils who they experience as difficult.

Through a shared understanding of the case, a child's disruptive behaviour can be understood as a message. Deciphering such messages leads to *changes in attitude* (Balint 1969) among teachers and educational professionals towards a child they experience as difficult. Understanding the message behind the child's disruptive behaviour enables teachers to maintain a professional distance. The disruptive behaviour, aggression or refusals are no longer experienced as personal provocations and insults.

Through case counselling or supervision, teachers are able to reflect on their own behaviour. Case counselling or supervision leads to a reflection of the relationship. Many factors and interdependencies from the school and extracurricular environment of the teacher and pupil can thus be recognised. This *change in attitude* opens up new space for manoeuvre for each individual in the multi-professional team.

In addition, case counselling and supervision relieve teachers and educational specialists emotionally, which is also a professional form of health promotion (Hehn-Oldiges 2021). For this reason, case counselling or supervision for the multi-professional team takes place regularly, ideally weekly, in the *Transition project*. It is important that the appointments are anchored in the school's weekly and annual calendar.

The case counselling can be moderated by the special needs teacher who is in charge of the *transition class*. It is also possible for the school psychology department or the regional inclusion education support system to take on this task. If the school management has a corresponding budget, supervision can also be financed via fee-based contracts.

The case study of *Janosch is* presented below. This is an example of how multi-professional case counselling can have a direct impact on the support and development of a child.

Janosch

The class teacher of a third primary school class presents a problem with a nine-year-old pupil in the case consultation. The teacher describes him as a boy with poor skills in all areas. He was also extremely slow, so she initially suspected that he had a need for support in the area of mental development. However, the diagnostics revealed age-appropriate intelligence and development in all areas.

The teacher reports that she tries to be patient with him and give him simple tasks. However, she notices that she avoids contact with him in class because his behaviour makes her angry. In the case consultation, she asks whether he would be better off going to a special school.

Other teachers also reported that his behaviour in class was in stark contrast to the results of the medical and psychological examinations. All the teachers noticed him because he moved challengingly slowly, like a snail. While all the other pupils had already finished working on a worksheet in class, he was still unzipping his pencil case to start his work. When the class teacher approaches him to ask him a lesson-related question, he seems absent and is unable to answer.

The class teacher has already had many discussions with the parents about the boy's problems and is convinced that more school support from the parents would help the boy to improve his performance in German and maths and change his behaviour.

The educational professionals from the after-school care centre report that he behaves in an age-appropriate manner there. He makes statements there about lesson content from class lessons that make it clear that he understands the lesson content and has achieved the competences, but obviously cannot present them in class.

The causes of the behaviour are identified in the case consultation: Both parents are very protective and overprotective of Janosch. He is treated like a toddler who can neither dress himself nor eat on his own. If his behaviour does not exactly meet his parents' expectations, he is dressed and sometimes even fed. Reflecting on the causes of parental behaviour would go too far here. Nevertheless, it can be said that his parents' fears of separation and control have the effect that he is kept dependent instead of being challenged in a manner appropriate to his age. His slowness represents the boy's resistance to this overprotection and is also an expression of his powerlessness in the face of his own parents.

In the classroom situation, the boy takes on a role that is very similar to his place within his family. In class, the boy transfers aspects of his father and mother onto the class teacher. Due to the existing *transference* and *countertransference,* the pupil's ego functions are characterised by powerlessness, listlessness and helplessness. This lack of drive is particularly evident in class. In after-school care, the boy has more freedom and can be active, learn and play.

The class teacher has previously experienced the pupil's slowness as a provocation. Through the case consultation, she can recognise the cause and understand the boy's behaviour. She recognises the pupil's powerlessness and helplessness and learns how to deal with him differently. The following solution is developed in the case counselling session: Janosch should learn to gradually become more independent and take on responsibility. The class teacher and a educational specialist from the after-school care centre give Janosch time every Monday to plan the implementation of the weekly tasks in a logbook. He then presents his plans to the class and receives feedback from previously nominated classmates. At the end of the week, a feedback meeting is held with him/her, the class teacher and a educational specialist from the after-school care centre to discuss the goals achieved. The feedback session begins with a self-assessment.

The change in the class teacher's *attitude* resulting from the case counselling is accompanied by a change in her attitude towards Janosch and her actions. This favours Janosch's positive development. The occurrence of such effects in the *Transition project* is favoured by regular (ideally weekly) case counselling and supervision in the team of teachers working with the child.

7.3.4 Counselling with parents

Chapter 5 already contains information on the topic of parental counselling for parents who teachers find difficult to reach. "Consultations with parents are very important, as they have a major impact on reducing behavioural problems in the classroom (…)" (Becker 2019b, 13). For this reason, parents are not only invited to individual meetings in the *Transition project,* but are also involved in a two-year process with regular joint counselling sessions. For this reason, the topic of *counselling with parents* is taken up again here and its importance and scope in the *Transition project* is presented in detail.

In the *Transition project,* counselling sessions between the teacher leading the temporary learning group *transition class* and the parents take place at least every 14 days or, if necessary, weekly or, in exceptional cases, daily. If parents are unable to come to the school, the counselling sessions are held in the form of home visits if the parents have no objections.

"In these discussions, the reasons for the childs abnormal behaviour are first discussed and the parents learn to understand the motives behind their child's disruptive behaviour. In this way, parents can change their attitude towards their child and it opens up a different perspective for them (…). This takes the pressure off the parent-child relationship and enables the parents to behave differently towards their child" (Becker 2008, 157).

It is of central importance for the success of counselling sessions with parents that they are able to talk about their individual problems first. This requires an inquisitive and appreciative attitude from the teacher. "The dialogue between teachers and parents usually has an immediate positive effect on the children's behaviour in class. As soon as the child senses the trusting cooperation between teachers and parents, the challenging behaviour in class is reduced. Surprisingly, this effect often occurs regardless of the topic of discussion between parents and teachers" (Becker 2019a, 13). It is important "that the child perceives the trusting cooperation between parents and teachers" (Becker 2019a, 13).

Artem

Artem (10) attends the fifth grade of a community school and has special educational needs in the area of emotional and social development. He also has fine motor difficulties, which contribute to his refusal to complete handwritten tasks. He appears very passive in class and often lies asleep with his head on his desk. When he does participate in class, he shows age-appropriate skills.

Artem's mother and stepfather work and are speechless in the face of Artem's challenging behaviour at school. They have him examined at a university clinic. He is diagnosed with a sensory integration disorder and a computer game disorder or *gaming disorder* according to ICD 11 (World Health Organisation 2019). Occupational therapy and psychotherapy are recommended and started as treatment.

During the parental interview, it becomes clear that the mother separated from Artem's father shortly after his birth because of his gambling addiction. She talks about her concern that Artem could become like his biological father. She says that she often reacted angrily or dismissively to him because of her fear.

Although the stepfather accompanies Artem to football training once a week, the boy's stepfather finds himself in a spectator position in relation to the relationship between his wife and the boy. The mother's concern that her son could become a gambling addict leads to her unintentionally comparing him to his biological father at school age, controlling him and unintentionally reinforcing the boy's problems with her attitude. For Artem, the computer game is a way out of a situation that is overwhelming him.

Once Artem's mother and stepfather understand the vicious circle in which the family finds itself, they begin to change their attitudes. In the conversations that follow, the parents learn that it is important to set limits for Artem and reduce the amount of time he spends playing on the computer. In the evenings, mum or stepdad now regularly take Artem swimming or play board games with him at home.

7.3.5 Cooperation between schools and youth welfare services

Children with special needs in their emotional and social development impairments in emotional and social development almost always require educational support. This refers to support measures to promote the parenting skills of parents and the participation opportunities of children and young people, which are outlined in the *Kinder- und Jugendhilfegesetz* [German Child and Youth Welfare Act] (SGB VIII). Section 27 (1) states: "A person with custody of a child or young person is entitled to help with the upbringing of a child or young person (educational assistance) if an upbringing that is in the child's or young person's best interests is not guaranteed and the help is suitable and necessary for their development" (Section 27 SGB VIII Art. 1) [translated by the author]. "This help can take the form of family support, a care assistant for the child, a socio-educational group or a day group" (Becker 2019a, 13) [translated by the author].

The youth welfare office becomes aware of children or young people in need when a child shows challenging behaviour in a day care centre, the parents already have help with upbringing in the family because of older siblings or teachers from a school report a child welfare risk to the youth welfare office. Another indication may be criminal offences reported to the police.

If support from the youth welfare office is suspected, a support conference is convened. This is where the necessity and type of help is decided. Help conferences are solution-orientated. If help is needed, the assistance is planned together with all stakeholders. This includes the parents, employees of an independent youth welfare organisation, the child and youth health service, the child psychiatric service, the educational counselling centre or the school psychology service. Children and young people are involved in an age-appropriate manner.

Even if teachers or educational specialists from a child's school often provide important information about a child to the youth welfare office, they can only be invited in exceptional cases for data protection reasons and to protect the privacy of the child and parents concerned. A school report on the child in question is often requested as input for the support conference. The school report is often a decisive factor in the choice of help. In this respect, it is very important that teachers or educational specialists at the school send these reports to the youth welfare office. As soon as educational support is installed in a family, it is very important for the success of the school support measures and educational support that school and non-school helpers co-operate with each other.

"School support conferences, collegial case consultations and support planning meetings focus on the individual support of children and young people. The feature film *Systemsprenger* (Fingscheidt 2019) is an example of how the lack of interaction between the institutions of youth welfare, health and school exacerbates the symptoms of the girl *Benny*. The film highlights the weaknesses of interdisciplinary cooperation. Conversely, successful cooperation between the various professional groups can make a decisive contribution to reducing symptoms in the area of behaviour. For this reason, case-related multi-professional cooperation is of great importance for the individual development of children and adolescents" (Becker 2022b, 64). "This close cooperation has a educational-therapeutic effect and often leads to a reduction in behavioural disorders in everyday school life" (Becker 2019a, 13).

Successful cooperation is therefore one of the five *learning accesses* within the *Transition project*. The cooperation concerns the everyday structure in the family and school, joint consultations with parents and the joint exchange between teachers and socio-educational specialists in youth welfare. It would be desirable for the socio-educational specialists from the independent youth welfare organisation to also take part in case consultations in the school's multi-professional team. However, this has often proved to be very difficult due to the different working time models. For example, the teachers have to teach the children in the morning and the socio-educational specialists have to provide educational support in the afternoon. Therefore, the areas of cooperation mentioned here are a supplement to case counselling in the multi-professional school team. The following forms of case-related co-operation have proven successful:

Daily handover between the class teacher and the caseworker

Cooperation leads to success as soon as the child experiences that all adults work together in everyday life. This has already been explained for multi-professional cooperation within schools and for counselling with parents and also applies to cooperation between schools and youth welfare services. Cooperation can become visible for younger children of primary school age when, for example, the caseworker picks up the child who attends a day group after school in the classroom. It is important that the caseworker and the teacher talk to each other and involve the child in an age-appropriate manner. The handover situation should not last longer than ten minutes and should include an exchange about how the child has worked hard in class and what tasks are to be completed in the afternoon. The walk from the school to the place where the educational support takes place should be used as a *educational walk* (Aichhorn 2005) to reflect on conflicts or problems with the child in an age-appropriate manner. In the case of older children or adolescents, a handover meeting between the teacher and the caseworker can also take place digitally.

Joint exchange

If necessary, consultations should take place between the caseworker from the independent youth welfare organisation and the teacher leading the *transition class* together with the parents in order to discuss the child's development, the multi-professional cooperation within the school and the duration of the child's participation in the temporary learning group in the *Transition project* and educational support. It is also about reflecting on the developmental steps of the last few weeks and discussing the next steps that are important for the child, the parents, the youth welfare organisation and the school. The child should be involved in an age-appropriate manner.

Depending on requirements, these consultations should take place at intervals of four, eight, twelve or 24 weeks. It is crucial to set the dates for one year at the beginning of the cooperation. It is always possible for all participants to postpone an appointment, but it is important for the attitude of all stakeholders towards cooperation to anchor this in the annual plan.

7.4 Conclusion

25 years of practical experience with the *Transition project* and the related studies (Becker 2008, 2012a, 2014, 2019) show that the situation for children, teachers, educational professionals and parents improves under the conditions of the five learning acccesses in such a way that inclusive education can succeed even in the case of special needs in the emotional and social development: For the schools involved in the empirical studies in Berlin, it was found that all children supported in the *Transition project* who were enrolled in a primary school – not a special school – were able to remain in their mainstream class (Becker 2008, 2014, 2019a). This requires a setting that creates space and time for relationship work at school.

8. Summary and outlook

8.1 Summary

In times of social crisis, as we have increasingly experienced since the start of the coronavirus pandemic in 2020, educational situations in the classroom and throughout the day are characterised by the social situation right down to the micro level of educational interactions. Even under these conditions, the principle of an appreciative attitude in educational relationships, in multi-professional cooperation and in joint counselling with parents applies. In this context, it is important to understand the concerns and needs of children and young people, their parents and teachers. These should be the starting point for educational action. This requires space and time for relationship work at school and in all-day programmes. In this book, solutions are developed on the basis of research and by analysing case studies. These can be divided into four dimensions:

Acting in educational emergency situations (short-term action)

Chapters 3 and 4 present case-specific solutions for difficult educational situations in which pupils harm themselves or others, which can be transferred to everyday school life in all types of schools.

Chapter 2 presents the so-called *Cuts,* ten tools developed and tested by the author of this book to de-escalate and end emergency situations in which pupils behave aggressively towards teachers or educational staff.

Plan and implement educational action in the medium term

For the medium-term planning and implementation of measures to support children or young people who express their worries and needs in challenging behaviour, advice is required on two levels:

- Joint counselling with the parents
- Regular case counselling or supervision in a multi-professional team

Prevent conflicts and challenging behaviour

The school policy and school rules play a key role in prevention. The school rules set a framework, just like the cushion in a game of pool. In this way, they show boundaries in school life and offer ways to intervene and make amends if rules are not adhered to.

Inclusive education for pupils with special needs in their emotional and social development

Children and young people with significant emotional and social impairments pose the greatest challenge for inclusive schools. In order for joint lessons with them to succeed, all stakeholders need to learn. The *Transition project* aims to achieve this with five *learning accessses* that enable mutual understanding and support for the children concerned. The *learning accesses* offer space and time for relationship work, which proves to be the key to the success of the inclusion of these pupils. In the *Transition project,* these five *learning accesses* are installed as fixed structures in everyday school life.

The case studies presented in this book illustrate that it is possible to find solutions to challenging behaviour that improve the situation for everyone involved. At the same time, the possible solutions presented here do not imply perfect or conflict-free developments. Behavioural problems remain a challenge for educational professionals, and all those involved will have to keep looking for solutions in the long term.

8.2 Outlook

In view of the results of the current IQB education trend (Stanat et al. 2022) and with a view to School 2030, education policy and academic discourse is primarily focused on the digitalisation of learning, the achievement of regular standards, sustainability and the safeguarding of basic mathematical and language skills. This is very important and, at the same time, a narrowing of the educational discourse must be avoided (Anders et al. 2023). For example, in the current debate as well as in initial, further and continuing education, a self-evident and very important level of action for the development of pupils is being neglected: the educational relationship.

Electricity, hydrogen, petrol or diesel are possible fuels for cars or other vehicles. Supportive relationships are the prerequisite and therefore the fuel for the development of a child's cognitive, emotional and social skills (Roorda et al. 2017). This is all the more true when children and young people grow up in difficult life situations.

In order to reflect on educational action in educational relationships in everyday teaching or all-day schooling, it is therefore important to offer regular case counselling or supervision in multi-professional year or school level teams, similar to the facilities of independent youth welfare organisations, and to firmly anchor this in a school's weekly or annual schedule. Time slots can be created for this through rhythmisation in the all-day school.

Research on the health of teachers shows that regular case counselling has a positive effect on the health of teachers. For example, Joachim Bauer developed the Freiburg model for the state of Baden-Württemberg, which is now available to all teachers there (Braeuning et al. 2018, Ministerium für Kultus, Jugend und Sport Baden-Württemberg 2022, Muenchhausen et al. 2021, Pfeifer et al. 2020, Pfeifer et al. 2021).

There are now similar programmes in many federal states of Germany, but they are usually only used by teachers if the school management actively promotes and supports them. In addition, it would be important for all stakeholders to give greater consideration to educational relationships as a topic in initial, continuing and further training. There are already positive examples of this:

The Rochow Academy in Brandenburg offers training courses on appreciative educational relationships for teachers in German-speaking countries (https://paedagogische-beziehungen.eu).

Additional information on the book series: *Educational Insights: Practice and Science in Dialogue can be found* at: https://paedagogischebeziehungen.eu/buchreihe-praxis-wissenschaft-dialog/.

The Helga Breuninger Foundation offers a video based empathy training for teachers to develop an open, agile mindset. This enables them to stay in conflicts present and empathic. (https://www.intushochdrei.de). Some of the case studies presented in this book were filmed by the Helga Breuninger Foundation as staged videos. They show teachers and educational professionals deescalating aggression by understanding and supporting their students . The training program: "Acting with presence and empathy in conflicts" is available in english. (https://www.intushochdrei.de/english)

With this book, I hope to make a contribution to improving school well-being, school learning and health promotion for all school stakeholders.

Literature

Adam, H. (2023) Krieg und Auswirkungen auf die Schule. Grundschule aktuell, Zeitschrift des Grundschulverbandes, 161, 15-16.

Adam, H./Bistritzky, H. (2017) Seelische Probleme von geflüchteten Kindern und Jugendlichen. Wie Schule und Kinderpsychiatrie kooperieren können. Berlin: Cornelsen Verlag.

Ahrbeck, B. (2007) Hyperaktivität. Kulturtheorie, Pädagogik, Therapie. Stuttgart: Kohlhammer Verlag.

Ahrbeck, B./Rauh, B. (Hrsg.) (2006) Der Fall des schwierigen Kindes. Therapie, Diagnostik und schulische Förderung verhaltensgestörter Kinder und Jugendlicher. Weinheim: Beltz Verlag.

Aichhorn, A. (1964) Delinquency and Child Guidance. Selected Papers. New York: International Universities Press.

Aichhorn, A. (2005) Verwahrloste Jugend (Nachdruck der 11. unveränderten Auflage 1987). Bern: Hans Huber Verlag.

Anders, P./Brinkmann, M./ Dietrich, C./Breidbach, S. (2023) Berliner Erklärung und offener Brief gegen eine Verengung des Bildungsdiskurses. In: Gesellschaft für Bildung Wissen e.V., Forum für Schule, Ausbildung und Studium (veröffentlicht am 19.04.2023). Available online: https://bildung-wissen.eu/fachbeitraege/berliner-erklaerung-und-offener-brief-gegen-eine-verengung-des-bildungsdiskurses.html (accessed on 3 Mai 2023).

Andresen, S./Lips, A./Möller, R./Rusack, T./Schröer, W./Thomas, S./Wilmes, J. (2020) Kinder, Eltern und ihre Erfahrungen während der Corona-Pandemie. Erste Ergebnisse der bundesweiten Studie KiCo. Hildesheim: Universitätsverlag Hildesheim. Available online: https://nbn-resolving.org/urn:nbn:de:gbv:hil2-opus410817 oder https://doi.org/10.18442/121 (accessed on 30 Mars 2023).

Andresen, S./Lips, A./Rusack, T./Schröer, W./Thomas, S./Wilmes, J. (2022) Verpasst? Verunschoben? Verunsichert? Erste Ergebnisse der JuCo III-Studie – Erfahrungen junger Menschen während der Corona-Pandemie im Winter 2021. Hildesheim: Universitätsverlag Hildesheim. Available online: https: https://nbn-resolving.org/ urn: nbn:de:gbv:hil2-opus4-13264 oder https://doi.org/10.18442/205 (accessed on 30 Mars 2023).

Auchter, T. (1994) Aggression als Zeichen von Hoffnung. In: Wege zum Menschen. Göttingen: Vandenhoeck & Ruprecht, 46, 2, 53-71.

Bachmair, S./Faber, J./Hennig, C./Kolb, R./Willig, W. (2014) Beraten will gelernt sein. Weinheim: Beltz Verlag.

Balint, M. (2018) Thrills and Regression. London: Taylor & Francis Group (first published 1959).

Balint, M. (1969) Ich-Stärke, Ich-Pädagogik und "Lernen". In: Urformen der Liebe. Bern: Hans Huber Verlag (first published 1938).

Balint, M. (1970) Therapeutische Aspekte der Regression. Die Theorie der Grundstörung. Stuttgart: Klett Verlag.

Bauer, J.(2020) Fühlen, was die Welt fühlt. München: Karl Blessing Verlag.

Becker, U. (1995a) Trennung und Übergang. Tübingen: edition discord.

Becker, U. (1995b) Lernen zwischen "Fort" und "Da". In: Becker, St. (Eds.), Helfen statt Heilen. Giessen: Psychosozial-Verlag, 177-183.

Becker, U. (2006) ADHS – Wo bleibt das Kind? In: Ahrbeck, B. (Eds.), Der Fall des schwierigen Kindes. Weinheim: Beltz Verlag, 160-180.

Becker, U. (2008) Lernzugänge. Wiesbaden: VS Verlag. doi: 10.1007/978-3-53191041-3.

Becker, U. (2010) Psychoanalytische Perspektiven der Behindertenpädagogik. In: Langnickel, R./Link, P.-C./Markowetz, R. (Eds.), Enzyklopädie Erziehungswissenschaft Online, Heil-, Sonder- und Inklusionspädagogik. Weinheim: Beltz Juventa Online. Available online: https://www.beltz.de/fachmedien/erziehungswissenschaft/enzyklopaedie_erziehungswissenschaft_online_eeo/artikel/9995-psychoanalytische-perspektiven-in-der-behindertenpaedagogik.html (accessed on 3 April 2023). doi: 10.3262/EEO11100083.

Becker, U. (2012a) Beeinträchtigungen im Sozialverhalten – eine Herausforderung für die inklusive Pädagogik. Vierteljahresschrift für Heilpädagogik und ihre Nachbarwissenschaften, 82, 3, 227-241.

Becker, U. (2012b) Von den Stärken ausgehen. In: Hansen-Schaberg, I./Schonig, B. (Eds.), Freinet-Pädagogik. Reformpädagogische Schulkonzepte, 5, 233-248.

Becker, U. (2014) Inclusive Education – Supporting Children with Behavioural Problems and Their Reference Persons in Lower Primary School. Journal of Special Education and Rehabilitation, 15, 1/2, 24-42. doi:10.2478/jser-2014-0002.

Spiewak, M. (2014): Du störst! Was tun mit einem Neuntklässler, der um sich schlägt? Ein Gespräch mit der Sonderpädagogin Ulrike Becker über verhaltensauffällige Schüler. Die ZEIT, Nr. 24 vom 5.6.2014, 71.

Becker, U. (2016a) Leben und Lernen in der Schulgemeinschaft – Schülerinnen und Schüler mit Verhaltensauffälligkeiten. In: Pädagogik, Themenheft "Verhaltensauffälligkeiten", 68, 11, 28-31.

Becker, U., Prengel, A. (2016b) Pädagogischen Beziehungen mit emotional-sozial beeinträchtigen Kindern und Jugendlichen – ein Beitrag zur Inklusion. In: Zimmermann, D./Meyer, M./Hoyer, J. (Eds.), Ausgrenzung und Teilhabe. Perspektiven einer kritischen Sonderpädagogik auf emotionale und soziale Entwicklung. Bad Heilbrunn: Klinkhardt Verlag, 94-104.

Becker, U. (2016c) Integrieren statt abschieben – schwierige Schüler erfolgreich in der inklusiven Schule unterrichten. In: Auf dem Weg zur inklusiven Schule, Praxisbegleiter für die Schulleitung. Stuttgart. Raabe Nachschlagen – Finden, 15, 1, 1-16.

Becker, U. (2019a) Jakob gehört zu uns!" "Schwierige" Schüler erfolgreich inklusiv unterrichten. In SCHULE inklusiv, 1, 2, 2019, 10-14.

Becker, U. (2019b) Alle Eltern erreichen. SCHULE inklusiv, 1, 5,15-20.

Becker, U. (2019c) Verhaltensauffälligkeiten. SCHULE inklusiv, 1, 2, 2019, 1014.

Becker, U./Brunswicker, K. (2020) Der mühevolle, aber gangbare Weg einer "Schule in schwieriger Lage" – der "Turnaround" am Beispiel einer Kreuzberger Sekundarschule. SCHULE inklusiv, 2, 7,10-14.

Becker, U. (2021a) Schule als sozialer Ort. SCHULE inklusiv, 3, 13, 2021, 13-16. Available online: https://www.friedrich-verlag.de/schulleitung/inklusion/ressourcen-nutzen-10391 (accessed on 15 Mars 2023).

Becker, U. (2021b) Schülerinnen und Schüler mit sonderpädagogischen Förderbedarfen. In: Seifried, K./Drewes, S./ Hasselhorn, M. (Eds.), Handbuch Schulpsychologie (3. überarb. und erw. Auflage). Stuttgart: Kohlhammer, 192-202.

Becker, U. (2022a) Projekt Übergang – Die temporäre Lerngruppe. Lecture on 7 October 2022 Landesinstitut für Schule Bremen.
Becker, U. (2022b) Multiprofessionelle Kooperation im Kontext inklusiver Bildung von Kindern und Jugendlichen mit Beeinträchtigungen in der emotionalen und sozialen Entwicklung. In: Serke, B./Streese, B. (Eds.), Wege der Kooperation im Kontext inklusiver Bildung. Bad Heilbrunn: Verlag Julius Klinkhardt 2022, 61-72. Available online: https://doi.org/10.35468/5958-07.
Becker, U. (2022c) Das Vertraute im Fremden sehen – Interkulturelle Konflikte lösen. In: Geflüchtete willkommen heißen. Hannover: Friedrich Verlag, 14-28.
Becker, U. (2023) Schülerinnen und Schüler mit traumatischen Erfahrungen im Projekt Übergang. Lecture on 23 mars 2023 Landesinstitut für Schule Bremen.
Berg, C. (1991) 1870-1918. Handbuch der deutschen Bildungsgeschichte, Band IV. München: C.H. Beck Verlag oHG.
Bergsson, M./Luckfiel, H. (1998) Umgang mit "schwierigen" Kindern. Berlin: Cornelsen-Scriptor.
Bernfeld, S. (1974) Der soziale Ort und seine Bedeutung für Neurosen, Verwahrlosung und Pädagogik. In: Werder, L./Wolff, R. (Eds.), Antiautoritäre Erziehung und Psychoanalyse II. Berlin: Ullstein TB Verlag.
Bless, G./Müller, C. (2017) Der Einfluss der Klassenkameraden auf Verhaltensprobleme. Zeitschrift für Heilpädagogik, 68, 12, 580-591.
Boller, S./Fabel-Lamla, M./Feindt, A./Kretschmer, W./Schnebel, S./Wischer, B. (2018): Kooperation. Friedrich Jahresheft XXXVI. Hannover: Friedrich Verlag.
Braeunig M./Pfeifer R./Schaarschmidt U./Lahmann C./ Bauer J (2018) Factors influencing mental health improvements in school teachers. doi: 10.1371/journal.pone.0206 412.
Bronfenbrenner, U. (1981) Die Oekologie der menschlichen Entwicklung. Stuttgart: Klett-Cotta Verlag.
Bronfenbrenner, U. (1994) Ecological models od human development. International Encyclopedia of Eduaction, Volume 3 (2nd Ed.). Oxford: Elsevier.
Bundesamtes für Migration und Flüchtlinge (2021) Das Bundesamt in Zahlen. Asyl. Im Internet unter: https://www.bamf.de/SharedDocs/Anlagen/DE/Statistik/Bun desamtin Zahlen/bundesamt-in-zahlen-2021-asyl.pdf?__blob=publicationFile&v =6 (accessed on 15 Mars 2022).
Bundeskriminalamt (2021): Vorstellung der Zahlen kindlicher Gewaltopfer – Auswertung der Polizeilichen Kriminalstatistik (PKS) 2020.
Correl, Christoph U. et al. (2022) A large-scale meta-analytic atlas of mental health problems prevalence during the COVID-19 early pandemic. Im Internet unter: https://www.ncbi.nlm.nih.gov/pmc/articles/PMC9015528/ (accessed on 12 February 2023).
DAK Gesundheit (2022) Kinder- und Jugendreport 2022.Available on: https:// www. dak.de/dak/gesundheit/kinder--und-jugendreport-2022-2571000.html#/ (accessed on 28 December 2022).
Depping, D./Lücken, M./ Musekamp, F./Thonke, M. (2021) Kompetenzstände Hamburger Schüler*innen vor und während der Corona-Pandemie. DDS- Die Deutsche Schule Beiheft 17, 51–79. Münster: Waxmann 2021. https://doi.org/10.31244/978 3830993315.03
Döttinger, I. (2018): Factsheet – Inklusion. Gütersloh: Bertelsmann Stiftung.

Dragioti E. Li H./Tsitsas G, et al. (2022): A large-scale meta-analytic atlas of mental health problems prevalence during the COVID-19 early pandemic. J Med Virol. 2022, 94, 1935-1949.

Ehlers, A. (2014) Regionale Kooperationen zwischen Schule und Jugendhilfe für die Bildung und Betreuung von Kindern und Jugendlichen mit besonders herausforderndem Verhalten. Lecture on 26 September 2014 in Hamburg.

Ehlers, A. (2023) Personal message in a telephone call about the *Transition project* in Hamburg (24 April 2023).

Engagement Global (2022) Ziele für nachhaltige Entwicklung. Im Internet unter: https://17ziele.de/ziele/1.html (accessed on 15. July 2022).

Engzell, P./Frey, A./Verhagen, M. D. (2020) Learning Inequality during the Covid-19 Pandemic. Available on: https://doi.org/10.31235/osf.io/ve4z7.

Erikson, E. H. (2021) Identität und Lebenszyklus. Frakfurt am Main: Suhrkamp Taschenbuch Verlag (first published 1973).

Faber, J. (2014) Gespräche mit Familien. In: Bachmair, S./Faber, J./Hennig, C./Kolb, R./Willig, W. (Eds.), Beraten will gelernt sein. Weinheim: Beltz Verlag, 87-91.

Fatke, R. (2022) Das "Life-Space Interview": Psychoanalytisch-pädagogisches Gespräch in Konfliktsituationen. In: Dörr, M./Kratz, M. (Eds.), Enzyklopädie Erziehungswissenschaft online: Psychoanalytische Pädagogik, ausgewählte Konzepte psychoanalytisch-pädagogischer Praxisgestaltung. Weinheim: Beltz Juventa, Online. Available online: https://www.beltz.de/fachmedien/erziehungswissenschaft/ enzyklopaedie_erziehungswissenschaft_online_eeo/artikel/50147-das-life-spaceinterview-psychoanalytisch-paedagogisches-gespraech-in-konfliktsituationen.html (accessed on 6 April 2023). doi: 10.3262/EEO19220463.

Federn, E. (1999) Ein Leben mit der Psychoanalyse. Gießen: Psychosozial Verlag.

Fingscheidt, N. (2019) Systemsprenger. Deutschland.

Fickermann, D./Edelstein, B. (2021) Schule während der Corona-Pandemie. Ein Überblick über Forschungsaktivitäten an Hand von Projektsteckbriefen. DDS – Die Deutsche Schule Beiheft 17, 103-212. Münster: Waxmann Verlag. Available online: https://doi.org/ 10.31244/9783830993315.

Fischer, Natalie/Richey, Petra (2021) Pädagogische Beziehungen für nachhaltiges Lernen. Stuttgart: Kohlhammer Verlag.

Freud, A. (2006) Das Ich und die Abwehrmechanismen (19. Aufl.). Frankfurt am Main: Fischer Verlag (first published 1936).

Freud, A. (1966) The Ego and the Mechanisms of Defence. London: Karnac Books.

Freud, S. (1920g) Beyond the Pleasure Principle. SE XVIII, 7-66. London: Hogarth Press 1953-1974.

Friedrichs, Birte (2023) Praxisbuch Klassenrat. Weinheim: Beltz Verlag.

Führ, C./Furck, C.-L. (1998) 1945 bis zur Gegenwart. Band VI. Handbuch der deutschen Bildungsgeschichte. München: C.H. Beck Verlag oHG.

Funcke, A./Menne, S. (2023) Kinderarmut in Deutschland. Factsheet. Gütersloh: Bertelsmannstiftung. Available online: https://www.bertelsmann-stiftung.de/filead min/files/ Projekte/Familie_und_Bildung/Factsheet_BNG_Kinder-_und_Jugendarmut_2023. pdf (accessed on 31 Mars 2023).

Gerbig, S./Feige, J. (2022) Das Wohl des Kindes bei Eltern in Haft – Recht auf Kontakt nach Artikel 9 der UN-Kinderrechtskonvention. In: Institut für Menschenrechte: Information 41. Available online: https://www.institut-fuer-menschenrechte.de/ fileadmin/Redaktion/Publikationen/Information/Information_Das_Wohl_des_Kindes_bei_Eltern_in_Haft.pdf (accessed on 8 April 2023).

Gerspach, M./Katzenbach, D. (1996) An der Szene teilhaben und doch innere Distanz dazu gewinnen. Behindertenpädagogik 35, 2, 354-372.

Gesamtschule Münster-Mitte: Schulprogramm. Available online: https://gesamtschule muenster.de/3-1-wie-wir-arbeiten-schulprogramm (accessed on 23 December 2022).

Geyer, M. (2004) Psychoanalytisch begründete Verfahren: Analytische und tiefenpsychologisch fundierte (psychodynamische) Psychotherapie. Available online: https://www.researchgate.net/profile/Michael-Geyer-5/publication/288174939_Psychoanalytisch_begrundete_Verfahren_Analytische_und_tiefenpsychologisch_fundierte_psychodynamische_Psychotherapie/links/5fcfa53d92851c00f85f04dc/Psychoanalytisch-begruendete-Verfahren-Analytische-und-tiefenpsychologischfundierte-psychodynamische-Psychotherapie.pdf (accessed on 6 April 2023).

Greiner, W./Batram, M./Witte, J. (2019) DAK Kinder- und Jugendreport 2019. Heidelberg: medhochzwei.

Günther, M./Bruns, G. (2010) Psychoanalytische Sozialarbeit. Stuttgart: Klett-Cotta Verlag.

Harris, A./Goodall, J. (2007) Engaging Parents in Raising Achievement. Do Parents Know They Matter? Warwick: University of Warwick.

Harris, A./Goodall, J. (2008) Do parents know they matter? Engaging all parents in learning. Educational Research, 50, 3, 277-289. Available online: https://doi.org/10.1080/00131880 802309424.

Havelmüller-Grundschule (2022): Schulprogramm. Available online: https://havel mueller-grundschule.de/wp-content/uploads/2020/05/Schulprogramm_2018.pdf (accessed on 23 December 2022).

Hehn-Oldiges, M./Piezunka, A./Prengel, A. (2020) Die "Reckahner Reflexionen zur Ethik pädagogischer Beziehungen" – Anregungen für die Umsetzung in die pädagogische Praxis. Behindertenpädagogik Heft 4/2020, S. 435-444.

Hehn-Oldiges, M. (2021) Wege aus Verhaltensfallen. Pädagogisches Handeln in schwierigen Situationen. Weinheim: Beltz Verlag.

Heinemann, E./Hopf, H. (2021) Psychische Störungen in Kindheit und Jugend. Stuttgart, Berlin, Köln: Kohlhammer Verlag.

Helbig, M. (2021) Lernrückstände nach Corona – und wie weiter? DDS – Die Deutsche Schule Beiheft 18, S. 127–146. Münster: Waxmann 2021. Available online: https://doi.org/10.31244/9783830994589.06.

Helga-Breuninger-Stiftung (2023) Potenzialentfaltung braucht den Potenzialblick. Ketzin: Sonderausgabe des Stiftungsmagazins NOOKEE.

Herz, B./Meyer, M./Liesebach, J. (2018) Integrationshelferinnen und Integrationshelfer in der schulischen Erziehungshilfe. In VHNplus, 87. Available online: www.reinhardt-journals.de/index.php/vhn/article/view/3266. (accessed on 14 Mars 2023).

Hirsch, Mathias. (1989) Der eigene Körper als Übergangsobjekt. In: Mathias Hirsch (Eds.), Der eigene Körper als Objekt. Zur Psychodynamik selbstdestruktiven Körperagierens. Berlin/Heidelberg/New York: Springer Verlag.

Hurrelmann, K./Rathmann, K. (2018) Leistung und Wohlbefinden in der Schule. Herausforderung Inklusion. Weinheim: Beltz Verlag.

Kaman, A./Erhart, M./ Devine, J./ Reiß, F./Napp, A.-K./Simon, A./Hurrelmann, K./ Schlack, R./Hölling, H./Wieler, L./Ravens-Sieberer, U. (2023) Two years of pandemic: the mental health and quality of life of children and adolescents – findings of

the COPSY longitudinal study. Dtsch Arztebl Int 2023, 120. doi: 10.3238/arztebl.m 2023.0001.
Kamm, C. (2022) Konzept Frei Day. Berlin. Senatsverwaltung für Bildung, Jugend und Familie.
Kamm, C./ Duveneck, T./ Hoffmeister, A./Becker U. (2023). "Stark trotz Corona": Aufwendig, aber erfolgreich!: Erfahrungen aus Berlin zum Bund-Länder-Programm "Aufholen nach Corona für Kinder und Jugendliche". DDS – Die Deutsche Schule, 115(4), 369-383. https://doi.org/10.31244/dds.2023.04.07
Katzenbach, D. (2004) Das Problem des Fremdverstehens. In: Wüllenweber, E. (Eds.), Soziale Probleme von Menschen mit geistiger Behinderung. Fremdbestimmung, Benachteiligung, Ausgrenzung und soziale Abwertung. Stuttgart: Kohlhammer Verlag, 322-334.
Kultusministerkonferenz (KMK) (2010) Dokumentation 189: Sonderpädagogische Förderung in Schulen 1999 bis 2008. Berlin 3, 2010.
Kultusministerkonferenz (KMK) (2013) Gemeinsame Erklärung der Kultusministerkonferenz und der Organisationen von Menschen mit Migrationshintergrund zur Erziehungs- und Bildungspartnerschaft von Schule und Eltern (resolution of the KMK on 10 October 2013).
Kultusministerkonferenz (KMK) (2016) Sonderpädagogische Förderung in Schulen 2005-2014. Berlin 2016.
Kultusministerkonferenz (KMK) (2018) Dokumentation 214: Sonderpädagogische Förderung in Schulen 2007-2016. Berlin 2, 2018.
Kultusministerkonferenz (KMK) (2018) Empfehlungen zur "Bildung und Erziehung als gemeinsame Aufgabe von Eltern und Schule" (resolution of the KMK on 11 October 2018).
Kultusministerkonferenz (KMK) (2020) Datensammlung Sonderpädagogische Förderung in allgemeinen Schulen 2017/2018 (Korrekturfassung vom 21.02.2020 – geänderte Daten im Blatt Quoten für die allgemeinen Schulen).
Kultusministerkonferenz (KMK) (2020) Datensammlung Sonderpädagogische Förderung in Förderschulen 2017/2018 (Korrekturfassung vom 21.02.2020 – geänderte Daten im Blatt Quoten für die allgemeinen Schulen).
Kultusministerkonferenz (KMK) (2020) Dokumentation 231: Sonderpädagogische Förderung in Schulen 2011-2020. Berlin 1/2022.
Kultusministerkonferenz (KMK) (2022) Junge Geflüchtete aus der Ukraine.Available online: https://www.kmk.org/fileadmin/Dateien/pdf/Statistik/Ukraine/AW_Uk raine _KW_14.pdf (accessed on 15 April 2022).
Kultusministerkonferenz (KMK) (2023) Geflüchtete Kinder/Jugendliche aus der Ukraine an deutschen Schulen. Available on: https://www.kmk.org/dokumentation-statistik/ statistik/schulstatistik/gefluechtete-kinderjugendliche-aus-der-ukraine.html (accessed on 07 April 2023).
Krowatschek, D./Krowatschek G./Reid, C. (2019) Marburger Konzentrationstraining. Dortmund: Verlag Modernes Lernen.
Lacan, J. (2002) Les complexes familiaux dans la formation de l'individu. Paris: L'Harmattan (first published 1938).
Langewiesche, D./Tenorth, H.-E. (1989) 1918-1945. Die Weimarer Republik und die nationalsozialistische Literatur. München: Verlag C.H. Beck oHG.
Langmeyer, A./Guglhör-Rudan, A./Naab, T./Urlen, M./Winklhofer, U. (2020a) Kind sein in Zeiten vor Corona. München: Deutsches Jugendinstitut e.V.

Langmeyer, A. (2020b) Mehr Kinder aus finanziell schlechter gestellten Familien fühlen sich einsam. Mitteilung des DJI zur Publikation der Studie: Kind sein in Zeiten von Corona. Available online: https://www.dji.de/veroeffentlichungen/pressemitteilungen/detailansicht/article/823-mehr-kinder-aus-finanziell-schlechter-gestellten-familien-fuehlen-sich-einsam.html (accessed on 10 Mars 2023).

Langnickel, R. (2021) Prolegomena zur Pädagogik des gespaltenen Subjekts. Ein notwendiger Riss in der Sonderpädagogik. Opladen, Berlin & Toronto: Verlag Barbara Budrich.

Langnickel, R./Link, P.-C., Markowetz, R. (2023) Enzyklopädie Erziehungswissenschaft Online. Heil-, Sonder- und Inklusionspädagogik. Available online: https://www.beltz.de/fileadmin/beltz/inhaltsverzeichnisse/eeo/Inhaltsverzeichnis_Heil-_Sonder-_und_Inklusionspaedagogik.pdf (accessed on 31 Mars 2023).

Leber, A. (1983) Reproduktion der frühen Erfahrung. Frankfurt am Main: Verlag Fachbuch für Psychologie.

Lempp, R. (2006) Die seelische Behinderung bei Kindern und Jugendlichen als Aufgabe der Jugendhilfe. Stuttgart: Richard Boorberg Verlag.

Lindemann, A./ Link, J.-W./ Prengel, A./Schmitt, H. (2020) Inklusive Tendenzen in der langen Geschichte der Grundschule – Historische Spurensuche zum 100-jährigen Bestehen der Grundschule. Pädagogische Rundschau 74, 1, 1–13.

Lütje-Klose, B./Urban, M. (2014) Professionelle Kooperation als wesentliche Bedingung inklusiver Schul- und Unterrichtsentwicklung. Teil 1: Grundlagen und Modelle inklusiver Kooperation. Vierteljahrsschrift für Heilpädagogik und ihre Nachbargebiete, 2, 112-128.

Luder, R. (2019) Auffälliges Verhalten in der Schule. Herausforderungen und Lösungsansätze. Vortrag an der Enquète "Schulklima – eine zeitgemäße Interpretation – Entwicklung von Lösungsansätzen für Verhaltensauffälligkeiten" (Lecture on 19 Mars 2019 in Vienna).

Luhmann, N. (1988a) Soziale Systeme. Frankfurt/Main, Suhrkamp Taschenbuch Verlag 1988.

Luhmann, N. (1988b) Ökologische Kommunikation. Opladen 1988.

Luhmann (1989) Ecological Communication. Chicago: University of Chicago Press,

Luhmann, N. (1995) Social Systems. Stanford: Stanford University Press.

Mannoni, M. (1982) D`un impossible à l`autre. Paris: Edition du Seuil.

Maurice, J./Will, G. (2021) Zentrale Befunde der Studie ReGES. Bericht Nr. 2 .Available online: https://www.lifbi.de/Portals/13/Transferberichte/LIfBi-Forschungskompakt_02_ReGES.pdf (accessed on 18 April 2022).

Maywald, J. (2019) Gewalt durch pädagogische Fachkräfte verhindern. Die Kita als sicherer Ort für Kinder. Freiburg: Herder Verlag.

Maywald, J. (2021) Gewaltzunahme gegenüber Kindern in der Corona-Pandemie. Personal message.

Mediendienst Integration (2023): Flüchtlinge aus der Ukraine. Available online: https://mediendienst-integration.de/migration/flucht-asyl/ukrainische-fluechtlinge.html (accessed on 1 April 2023).

Medvedev, A. (2020) Heterogene Eltern. Die Kooperation von Eltern und Schule neu denken und umsetzen. Neue Wege der Elternkooperation. Weinheim: Beltz Verlag.

Ministerium für Kultus, Jugend und Sport Baden-Württemberg (2022) LehrerCoachinggruppen nach dem Freiburger-Modell. Available online: https://arbeits schutz-sch ule.kultus-bw.de/,Lde/Startseite/Aktuelles/Lehrer-Coachinggruppen+Freiburger+M odell (accessed on 31 December 2022).

Muenchhausen, S./von/Braeunig, M./Pfeifer, R./Göritz, A. S./Bauer, J./Lahmann, C./ Wuensch, A. (2021) Teacher Self-Efficacy and Mental Health – Their Intricate Relation to Professional Resources and Attitudes in an Established Manual-Based Psychological Group Program. Frontiers in Psychiatry, 12. https://doi.org/10.3389/fpsyt.2021.510183.

Nassehi, A. (2022). Der Mensch täuscht sich meistens selbst. In: Tagesspiegel vom 16.04.2022, 4.

Nassehi, A./Nollmann, G. (2016): Bourdieu und Luhmann. Ein Theorienvergleich. Frankfurt/Main: Suhrkamp Verlag.

Nationales Zentrum frühe Hilfen (2022): Zahlen und Fakten zum Schütteltrauma. Available online: https://www.fruehehilfen.de/grundlagen-und-fachthemen/fachthemen/babyschreien-und-schuetteltrauma/zahlen-und-fakten (accessed on 15 June 2022).

Oswald, H. (2009) Persönliche Beziehung in der Kindehit. In: Lenz, K./Nestmann, F. (Eds.), Handbuch Persönliche Beziehungen. Weinheim und München: Juventa Verlag, 491-512.

Paar, Gerhard H. (1987) Selbstzerstörung als Selbsterhaltung: Eine Untersuchung zu Patienten mit artifiziellen Syndromen. Materialien zur Psychoanalyse und analytisch orientierten Psychotherapie, Volume 13, 1, 1-54.

Pech, D. (2018) Beobachten, ausprobieren, ordnen und erkunden. Vom Umgehen mit der Welt als Erkenntnisgewinn. In: Grundschule Sachunterricht, 79, 2018, 12-15.

Pech, D. (2020) Tragfähige Grundlagen. Sachunterricht. In : Hecker, U./Lassek, M./ Ramseger, J. (Eds.), Anforderungen und tragfähige Grundlagen. Kinder lernen Zukunft. Beiträge zur Reform der Grundschulpädagogik, Volume 150. Frankfurt am Main: Grundschulverband, 158-167.

Peirce, Ch. S. (1987) Collected Papers of Charles Sanders Peirce (edited by Charles Hartshorne, Paul Weiss, and Arthur W. Burks 1931-1958). Harvard University Press, Cambridge, Massachusetts.

Peirce, Ch. S. (2016) Schriften zum Pragmatismus und Pragmatizismus (3. Auflage 2016). Frankfurt am Main. Suhrkamp Verlag (first published 1903).

Pfeifer, R./Matthiessen, J./Braeunig, M./ Göritz, A.S./Lahmann, C./Bauer, J./ Wünsch, A. (2020): Erfolgreiches Coaching für Lehrer/innen zur Förderung der Beziehungskompetenz – das "Freiburger Modell" unter der Lupe. Eine qualitative Studie zu Wirkfaktoren, Transferleistung und Schlüsselmomenten einer Maßnahme zu Förderung und Erhalt der Lehrer/innen-Gesundheit. Lehren & Lernen, 8/92020, 39-47.

Pfeifer, R./ Braeunig, M./Wünsch, A. (2021) Beziehungen im Schulalltag gestalten – Eine Herausforderung für Lehrer/innen gerade in Zeiten der Corona-Pandemie. Lehren & Lernen, 47, 5, 32-33. Available online: https://neckar-verlag.de/schule/lehren-lernen/ausgaben-downloads/2644/beziehungen-im-schulalltag-gestalten?c=89 (accessed on 06 Mars 2022).

Piezunka, A. (2020) Gestaltung pädagogischer Beziehungen: Partizipation ermöglichen. In: Boban, I./Hinz, A. (Eds.), Inklusion und Partizipation – Herausforderungen für Schule. Theoretische Analysen, methodische Überlegungen, praktische Beispiele. Weinheim, Basel: Julius Klinkhardt Verlag.

Prengel, A. (2005) Anerkennung von Anfang an – Egalität, Heterogenität und Hierarchie im Anfangsunterricht und darüber hinaus. In: Geiling, U./Hinz, A. (Eds.), Integrationspädagogik im Diskurs. Bad Heilbrunn: Klinkhardt Verlag, 15-34.

Prengel, A. (2008) Anerkennung als Kategorie pädagogischen Handelns. Theorie und Vision einer anderen Schulkultur. In: Pädagogik: Respekt und Anerkennung. 60, 2, 33-35.

Prengel, A. (2012) Die Lehrer-Schüler-Beziehung aus menschenrechtlicher Sicht analysieren – Vorschläge für Lehr-Forschungsprojekte. Zeitschrift für Menschenrechtsbildung. Bern: Stämpfli Verlag. 4,1, 26-28.

Prengel, A. (2012) Anerkennung in Lehrer-Schüler-Beziehungen als Bedingung sozialen und kognitiven Lernens. In: Hellmich, F./Förster,S./Hoya, F. (Eds.), Bedingungen des Lehrens und Lernens in der Grundschule. Bilanz und Perspektiven. Wiesbaden. 73-76.

Prengel, A./Winklhofer U. (Hrsg.) (2014) Kinderrechte in Pädagogischen Beziehungen. Volume 1: Praxiszugänge. Volume 2. Forschungszugänge. Opladen/Berlin/Toronto: Barbara Budrich Verlag.

Prengel, Annedore (2016a):Pädagogische Beziehungen im Lichte der Kinderrechte. In: Krappmann, L./Petry, C. (Eds.), Worauf Kinder und Jugendliche ein Recht haben. Kinderrechte, Demokratie und Schule: Ein Manifest. Schwalbach: Debus Pädagogik, 149-161.

Prengel, A. (2016b) Bildungsteilhabe und Partizipation in Kindertageseinrichtungen. München: Deutsches Jugendinstitut e.V./Weiterbildungsinitiative Frühpädagogische Fachkräfte (WiFF).

Prengel, A. (2017) Reckahner Reflexionen zur Ethik pädagogischer Beziehungen. Reckahn: Rochow-Akademie. Available online: https://paedagogische-beziehungen.eu (accessed on 15 Mars 2022).

Prengel, A. (2017) Reckahner Reflections on the Ethics of Educational Relations. Available online: https://paedagogische-beziehungen.eu/wp-content/uploads/2018/01/RZ_ohneBeschnitt_Englisch_Reckahner_Reflektionen_flyer.pdf (accessed on 8 August 2023).

Prengel, A. (2018): Relation. In: Blohm, M./ Brenne, A./Hornäk, S. (Eds.), Irgendwie anders. Inklusionsaspekte in den künstlerischen Fächern und der ästhetischen Bildung. Flensburg: Fabrico Verlag, 55-60.

Prengel, A. (2019) Pädagogik der Vielfalt. Verschiedenheit und Gleichberechtigung in Interkultureller, Feministischer und Integrativer Pädagogik. Wiesbaden: Springer VS.

Prengel, A. (2019). Pädagogische Beziehungen zwischen Anerkennung, Verletzung und Ambivalenz. Opladen/Berlin/Toronto: Barbara Budrich. Available online: https://doi.org/10.2307/j.ctvh1dpbj.

Prengel, A./Maywald, J.(2020) Reckahner für große und kleine Kinder. Reckahn: Rochow Akademie & Pädagogische Hochscule Steiermark. Im Internet unter: https://paedagogische-beziehungen.eu/regelbuechlein-2/ (Zugriff am 01.04. 2023).

Prengel, A. (2020) Ethische Pädagogik in Kitas und Schulen.Weinheim/Basel: Beltz Verlag.

Prengel, A. (2021) Auf die Beziehungen kommt es an! Kinderrechte als gemeinsame Basis multiprofessionellen relationalen Handeln. In: Hoffmann, I./Köhler, B. (Eds.), verschieden* gleich* gemeinsam. Zusammenarbeit in multiprofessionllen Teams. Frankfurt am Main: Gewerkschaft Erziehung und Wissenschaft, 7-13.

Prengel, A. (2021) Relationentheorien und ihre Bedeutung für die Pädagogikethik. In: Ebner von Eschenbach, M./Schäffter, O. (Eds.), Denken in wechselseitiger Beziehung: Das Spectaculum relationaler Ansätze in der Erziehungswissenschaft. Weilerswist: Velbrück Verlag, 259-285.

Prengel, A. (2021) Der furchtbare Moment im Bildungsprozess. Elemente einer Theorie destruktiver pädagogischer Relationalität. In: Hagenauer, G./Raufelder, D. (Eds.), Soziale Eingebundenheit. Sozialbeziehungen im Fokus von Schule und Lehrer*innenbildung. Münster: Waxmann Verlag, 57-70.

Prengel, A. (2021) Die "Reckahner Reflexionen zur Ethik pädagogischer Beziehungen" – ein Beitrag zur Demokratie als Lebensform. In: Demokratiebildung. Politik und Wirtschaft unterrichten Sonderausgabe Sekundarstufe I / II, Wochenschau 72. Jg. Juli 2021, 22-24.

Prengel, A. (2021) Alle Formen von Gewalt an kleinen Kindern sichtbar machen – Ein Wort zum Geleit. In: Boll, A./Remsperger-Kehm, R. (Eds.), Verletzendes Verhalten in Kitas. Opladen: Barbara Budrich Verlag , 5-6.

Prengel, A. (2022) Schulen inklusiv gestalten eine Einführung in Gründe und Handlungsmöglichkeiten. Opladen: Barbara Budrich Verlag.

Ramseger, J. (2019) Grundschule 2030: Was bleiben wird und was sich ändern könnte. Abschlussvortrag zum Bundesgrundschulkongress am 14.9.2019 in der GoetheUniversität Frankfurt am Main. Available online: https://grundschulverband.de/ wp-content/uploads/2019/11/Abschlussvortrag-BGK-2019_Jörg-Ramseger.pdf (accessed on 06 April 2023).

Rasfeld, M. (2021): Frei Day. München: Oekom Verlag.

Ravens-Sieberer, U./Kaman, A./Otto, C. et al. (2021) Seelische Gesundheit und psychische Belastungen von Kindern und Jugendlichen in der ersten Welle der COVID-19-Pandemie – Ergebnisse der COPSY-Studie. In: Bundesgesundheitsbl 64, 1512–1521 (2021). Available online: https://doi.org/10.1007/s00103-021-03291-3.

Ravens-Sieberer, U./Kaman, A./Devine, J./Löffler, C./Reiß, F./Napp, A. K./ Gilbert, M./Naderi, H./Hurrelmann, K./Schlack, R./Hölling, H./Erhart, M. (2022a) The mental health and health-related behavior of children and parents during the COVID-19 pandemic: findings of the longitudinal COPSY study. In: Dtsch Arztebl Int 2022; 119. doi: 10.3238/arztebl.m2022.0173 (online first).

Ravens-Sieberer, U, Kaman, A. et al. (2022b) Child and adolescent mental health during the COVID-19 pandemic: Results of the three-wave longitudinal COPSY study. Preprint. Available online: http://ssrn.com/abstract=4024489 (accessed on 06 Mars 2022).

Ravens-Sieberer, U./Kaman, A./Devine, , C./Reiß, F./Napp, A. K./ Gilbert, M./Naderi, H./Hurrelmann, K./Schlack, R./Hölling, H./Erhart, M./Saftig, L./Reiss, F./Löffler, C./Simon, A./ Hurrelmann, K./Walper, S./Wieler, L. H. (2022c) Three Years into the Pandemic: Results of the Longitudinal German COPSY Study on Youth Mental Health and Health-Related Quality of Life (16 December 2022). Available online: https://ssrn.com/abstract=4304666 or http://dx. doi.org/10.2139/ssrn.4304666 (accessed on 6 April 2023).

Reckwitz, A. (2020) Das Ende der Illusionen. Politik, Ökonomie und Kultur in der Spätmoderne. Berlin: Suhrkamp (edition suhrkamp).

Refik-Veseli-Schule (2017): School Handbook. Available online: https://www.refik-veseli-schule.eu/cms/_ rubric/index.php/home (accessed on 23 December 2022).

Rjosk, C./Richter, D./Hochweber, J./Lüdtke, O./Stanat, P. (2015) Classroom composition and language minority students' motivation in language lessons. Journal of Educational Psychology, 107, 1171–1185. doi: 10.1037/edu0000035.

Robert-Bosch-Stiftung (2022) Der Deutsche Schulpreis. Available online: https:// www.deutscher-schulpreis.de (accessed on 23 December 2022).

Robert-Koch-Institut (2018): KiGGS Welle 2 – Erste Ergebnisse aus Querschnitt- und Kohortenanalysen. Journal of Health Monitoring, 3, 1, 2018. doi: 10.17886/ RKI-GBE-2018-003.

Roorda, D. L./Jak, S./Zee, M./Oort, F. J./Koomen, H. M. Y. (2017) Affective Teacher–Student Relationships and Students' Engagement and Achievement. A Meta- Analytic Update and Test of the Mediating Role of Engagement. School Psychology Review, 46, 3, 239-261. Available online: https://doi.org/10.17105/SPR-2017-0035.V 46-3.

Sacher, W. (2012) Schule: Elternarbeit mit schwer erreichbaren Eltern. In: Stange, W./Krüger, R./Henschel, A./Schmitt, C. (Eds.), Erziehungs- und Bildungspartnerschaften. Wiesbaden: Springer VS, 297-303.

Sachsse, U. (1987) Selbstbeschädigung als Selbstfürsorge. Zur intrapersonalen und interpersonellen Psychodynamik schwerer Selbstbeschädigungen der Haut. Forum Psychoanalyse, 3, 51-70.

Sachsse, U. (1989) "Blut tut gut". Genese, Psychodynamik und Psychotherapie offener Selbstbeschädigungen der Haut. In: Mathias Hirsch (Eds.), Der eigene Körper als Objekt. Zur Psychodynamik selbstdestruktiven Körperagierens. Berlin/Heidelberg/New York: Springer Verlag.

Sachsse, U. (1994) Selbstverletzendes Verhalten. Psychodynamik – Psychotherapie. Göttingen/Zürich: Vandenhoeck und Ruprecht.

Santen, E. v./Seckinger, M. (2017) Kooperation und Konflikt. In: Kessl, F./Kruse, E./Stövesand, S./Thole, W. (Eds.): Soziale Arbeit – Kernthemen und Problemfelder. Opladen und Toronto: Verlag Barbara Budrich, 194-201.

Santen, E. v. (2021) Interinstitutionelle Kooperation – Eine boomende Strategie. Sozialpädagogische Impulse, 2, 12-14.

Scherzinger, M./Wettstein, A. (2022) Beziehungen in der Schule gestalten. Für ein gelingendes Miteinander. Stuttgart: Kohlhammer Verlag.

Schiffauer, W. (2015) Schule, Moschee, Elternhaus. Eine ethnologische Intervention. Berlin: Suhrkamp Verlag.

Schule im Aufbruch (2022) Frei Day. Available online: https://schule-im-aufbruch.de/ netzwerke/netzwerk-frei-day (accessed on 15 July 2022).

Schulz, L. (2021) Feedback im digital-inklusiven Unterricht. Lernprozesse erfolgreich begleiten. Stuttgart: Raabe-Verlag.

Seifried, K./Drewes, S./Hasselhorn, M. (2021) Handbuch Schulpsychologie – Psychologie für die Schule. Stuttgart. Kohlhammer Verlag.

Seifried, K. (2021) Kinder und Jugendliche mit psychischen Erkrankungen – eine Aufgabe der inklusiven Schule (2021). In: Seifried, K./Drewes, S./Hasselhorn, M. (Eds.):,Handbuch Schulpsychologie. Stuttgart. Kohlhammer Verlag, 285-297.

Seifried, K. (2021a) Beratung in der Schule – Kooperation und Vernetzung. In: Seifried, K./Drewes, S./Hasselhorn, M. (Eds.), Handbuch Schulpsychologie (3. überarb. Aufl.). Stuttgart: Kohlhammer Verlag, 56-71.

Seifried, K. (2021b) Die inklusive Schule – Ein Aufgabenfeld der Schulpsychologie. In: Seifried, K./Drewes, S./Hasselhorn, M. (Eds), Handbuch Schulpsychologie. Stuttgart: Kohlhammer Verlag, 285-297

Seifried, K. (2021c) Supervision und Coaching in der Schule. In: Seifried, K./Drewes, S./Hasselhorn, M. (Eds.), Handbuch Schulpsychologie. Stuttgart: Kohlhammer Verlag.

Senatsverwaltung für Bildung, Jugend und Familie (2021): Rahmenkonzept "Stark trotz Corona" – Bund-Länderprogramm zum Aufholen nach Corona für Kinder und Jugendliche. Available online: https://www.berlin.de/sen/bjf/stark-trotz-coro na/ (accessed on 31 Mars 2023).

Serke, B./Streese, B. (2022) Wege der Kooperation im Kontext inklusiver Bildung. Wege der Kooperation im Kontext inklusiver Bildung. Bad Heilbrunn: Verlag Julius Klinkhardt. Available online: https://www.pedocs.de/volltexte/2022/24881/ pdf/Serke_Str eese_2022_Wege_der_Kooperation.pdf (accessed on 28 November 2022). doi: 10. 25656/01:24881.

Streese, B./Werning, R. (2021) Beratung. SCHULE inklusiv, 3, 12.

Sozialgesetzbuch Achtes Buch (SGB VIII) – Kinder- und Jugendhilfe, zuletzt geändert durch Art. 1 G v. 21.12.2022.

Stanat, P./Schipolowski, S./Schneider, R./Sachse, K.A./Weirich, S./Henschel, S. (Eds.) (2022), IQB-Bildungstrend 2021. Kompetenzen in den Fächern Deutsch und Mathematik am Ende der 4. Jahrgangsstufe im dritten Ländervergleich. Münster/New York: Waxmann Verlag. doi: 10.31244/9783830996064.

Stange, W. (2012) Erziehungs- und Bildungspartnerschaften – Grundlagen, Strukturen, Begründungen. In: Erziehungs- und Bildungspartnerschaft. Wiesbaden: VS Verlag für Sozialwissenschaften/Springer Fachmedien, 12-39. doi: 10.1007/9783-531-94 279-7.

Statistische Ämter des Bundes und der Länder (2022) Gemeinsames Statistikportal. Armutsgefährdungsquote nach soziodemografischen Merkmalen in Prozent gemessen am Bundesmedian. Available online: https://www.google.com/search?cli ent=safari&rls=en&q=Armutsgefährdung%7CStatistikportal.de&ie=UTF-8&oe=UTF-8 (accessed on 31 Mars 2023).

Statista (2023) Schätzungen der Gesamtanzahl der Flüchtlinge aus der Ukraine nach Grenzübertritten in Folge des Krieges von Februar 2022 bis Januar 2023. Statista, 24.1.2023. Available online: https://de.statista.com/statistik/daten/studie/1293762/ um frage/anzahl-der-kriegsfluechtlinge-aus-der-ukraine/ (accessed on 31 January 2023).

Tellisch, C./Ostermann, B. (2021) Bildung, Pandemie, Herausforderungen: Hybridität als Lösung?. Bonn: Verlag für Kultur und Wissenschaft.

Tenorth, H.-E. (2019) Begründung der Schulpflicht. In: Drerup, J./Schweiger, G. (Eds.), Handbuch Philosophie der Kindheit. Stuttgart: J.B. Metzler, 419-439.

Teubert, K. (1997) "Ich blute, also bin ich": Aspekte autoaggressiven Hautritzens bei Mädchen und jungen Frauen. Psychologie und Gesellschaftskritik, 21, 2 , 5-28. Available online: https://nbn-resolving.org/urn:nbn:de:0168-ssoar-290678 (accessed on 16 Mars 2022).

Thiersch, H. (2020) Lebensweltorientierte soziale Arbeit. Weinheim: Beltz Verlag.

Theunissen, G./Kulig, W. (2015) KVJS-Forschungsprojekt "Menschen mit geistiger oder mehrfacher Behinderung und sogenannten herausfordernden Verhaltensweisen in Einrichtungen der Behindertenhilfe in Baden-Württemberg" Gesamtbericht der Martin-Luther-Universität Halle-Wittenberg.Halle-Wittenberg: Kommunalverband für Jugend und Soziales Baden-Württemberg.

Ulrich, B. (2022) Sieben auf einen Streich. Artensterben, Klimawandel, Corona, Krieg, Hunger, Massenflucht aus Ost und Süd: Die Krisen sind so eng verzahnt, dass es kein Zurück zur Normalität gibt. ZEIT, 13, 2022.

UN General Assembly (1989) Convention on the rights of the child. General Assembly resolution 44/25. Available online: https://www.ohchr.org/en/instruments-mechanisms/instruments/convention-rights-child (accessed on 5 February 2022).
UN General Assembly (2007) Convention on the Rights of Persons with Disabilities. Resolution adopted by the General Assembly A/61/611. Available online: https://www.refworld.org/legal/resolution/unga/2007/en/49751 (accessed on 25 February 2022).
UNHCR (2023a) Statistiken. Available online: https://www.unhcr.org/dach/de/services/statistiken. (accessed on 31 January 2023).
UNHCR (2023b) UNHCR Data. Available online: https://www.unhcr.org/what-we-do/reports-and-publications/unhcr-data (accessed on 5 February 2023).
UNICEF (1989) Konvention über die Rechte von Kindern. Available online: https://www.unicef.de/informieren/ueber-uns/fuer-kinderrechte/un-kinderrechtskonvention (accessed on 15 July 2022).
UNICEF (2016) The growing crisis for refugee and migrant children. Available online: https://data.unicef.org/resources/uprooted-growing-crisis-refugee-migrant-children/ (accessed on 15 April 2022).
UNICEF (2020) Child Migration. Available online: https://data.unicef.org/topic/child-migration-and-displacement/migration/ (accessed on 15 April 2022).
UNICEF (2021) Impact of COVID-19 on poor mental health in children and young people 'tip of the iceberg'. Available online: https://www.unicef.org/press-releases/impact-covid-19-poor-mental-health-children-and-young-people-tip-iceberg (accessed on 15 Mars 2022).
UNICEF (2022) Fast zwei Drittel der ukrainischen Kinder auf der Flucht. Available online: https://www.deutschlandfunk.de/fast-zwei-drittel-der-ukrainischen-kinderauf-der-flucht-100.html (accessed on 15 April 2022).
Urban, M. (2021) Sichere Orte in der Schule. SCHULE inklusiv, 3, 13, 8-12.
Urban, M./Lütje-Klose, B. (2014) Professionelle Kooperation als wesentliche Bedingung inklusiver Schul- und Unterrichtsentwicklung. Teil 2: Forschungsergebnisse zu intra- und interprofessioneller Kooperation. Vierteljahresschrift für Heilpädagogik und ihre Nachbargebiete, 4, 283-294.
World Health Organization (WHO) (2019) ICD-11: International Classification of Diseases, 11thRevision. The global standard for diagnostic health information. Available online: https://www.bfarm.de/DE/Kodiersysteme/Klassifikationen/ICD/ICD-11/_node.html (accessed on 29 December 2022).
Werning, R. (2015) Umgehen mit Unterrichtsstörungen. Pädagogische Handlungsmöglichkeiten unter systemischer Perspektive. In: Bietz, C. et.al. (Eds.), Unterrichtsstörungen. Friedrich Jahresheft XXXIII, Seelze, 31-33.
Werning, R./Lichblau, M. (2020) Schulische Inklusion in den Bundesländern. Bildungspolitische Entscheidungen und Quoten im Vergleich. Pädagogik 72, 4, 43-47.
Werning, R. (2022) Kooperation von professionellen Akteur*innen in inklusiven pädagogischen Settings – der Beitrag von Birgit Lütje-Klose. In: Serke, B./Streese, B. (Eds.), Wege der Kooperation im Kontext inklusiver Bildung. Bad Heilbrunn: Verlag Julius Klinkhardt. Available online: https://www.pedocs.de/volltexte/2022/24881/pdf/Serke_Streese_2022_Wege_der_Kooperation.pdf (accessed on 28 November 2022). doi: 10.25656/01:24881.
Winnicott, D.W. (1965): The maturational processes and the facilitating environment. London: International Universities Press.
Winnicott, D. W. (2005) Playing and Reality (2nd Ed.). London: Routledge.

Winnicott, D. W. (2020) Hate in the counter-transference. The International Journal of Psychoanalysis, 30, 69-74.
Winnicott, D.W. (2023): Reifungsprozesse und fördernde Umwelt (4. Auflage). Gießen: Psychosozial-Verlag (first published 1965).
Wood, M.M. (1996) Developmental Therapy – Developmental Teaching. TX: Pro-Ed. Austin.
Wuntke, L.V./Blumenthal, Y./Köhler, J./Mahlau, K. (2023) (Eds.), Das Familienklassenzimmer. Zeitschrift für Heilpädagogik, 74, 4, 2023, 148-155.
Würker, A. (2007) Lehrerbildung und Szenisches Verstehen. Baltmannsweiler: Schneider-Verlag.
Zimmermann, D. (2021) Traumatisierung und Schule. SCHULE inklusiv, 3, 13, 2-7.
Zimmermann, D./Würker, A. (2023): Entgrenzungen und Begrenzungen. Pychoanalytisch-pädagogische Einsichten. psychosozial 172 (46/2). Gießen: Psychosozial.

Index

basic disorder 83
challenging behaviour 11f., 17, 20, 22, 24f., 27-30, 40, 51, 65, 68, 70f., 74-77, 79, 81, 83, 85f., 92f., 96f.
children's rights 18, 78
closeness and distance 20-22, 25, 55, 61
counselling 5, 12, 29f., 42, 52, 55, 58f., 61, 63, 68-70, 84-86, 89, 91, 93f., 96f.
counselling with parents 12, 64, 86, 91, 94, 96
cut 32, 38, 57, 88
educational relationships 20-22, 81, 83, 96-98
Helga Breuninger Foundation 11, 13, 98
hyperactivity 58
inclusive teaching 86

learning accesses 81f., 85f., 94, 97
Reckahn Reflections on the Ethics of Educational Relations 38, 78
reparation instead of punishment 30, 38
school policy 12, 39, 75-77, 79, 96
school rules 12, 30, 32, 38f., 50, 75, 77-79, 96
scratching 52, 56-58
separation anxiety 54f.
temporary learning group 59, 82-87, 92, 95
transference 28, 91
Transition project 82-84, 86-88, 90-92, 94f., 97
transitional object 81
welfare services 30, 63, 82, 85f., 94

Claudia Equit (ed.)

Participation in Residential Childcare

Safeguarding children's rights through participation and complaint procedures

2024 • 255 pp. • Pb. • 54,90 € (D) • 56,50 € (A)
ISBN 978-3-8474-2709-4 • eISBN 978-3-8474-1879-5 (Open Access)

Article 12 of the UN Convention on the Rights of the Child establishes the right to participation: children and adolescents are entitled to participate and to have their views taken into account in all issues affecting them in accordance to their age and maturity. The volume explores this right to participation in residential care. The impact of participation and complaint procedures in residential care facilities are evaluated by means of crucial results from an empirical study. How do these participation and complaints procedures work? The authors discuss crucial facilitators and barriers with regard to the implementation of children's rights to participate.

www.shop.budrich.de